CW01019444

The Life of
Arnold Freeman

Philosopher, Teacher and Social Reformer

Arnold as a young man.

The Life of
Arnold Freeman

Philosopher, Teacher and Social Reformer

Kenneth Gibson

**Wynstones
Press**

Published by
Wynstones Press
Stourbridge
England.

www.wynstonespress.com

First edition 2023

Printed by Gutenberg Press, Malta.

ISBN 9780 946206 99 5

Contents

Chapter Five: Spiritualism and Theosophy

Chapter Six: The Guru

Chapter Seven: A Working Life

Chapter Eight: The Great War, Writing and Reconstruction

Chapter Nine: Building a New Society

Preface

When the Ruskin Mill Trust chose Sheffield as its third further education college for learners with special educational needs, the legacy of Arnold Freeman provided a firm foundation on which to build. The emphasis of Freeman's approach was on the cultural performance of students rather than their work performance. Sheffield had been defined by John Ruskin in the following words: 'In Cutlers Iron Works, we have in Sheffield the best of its kind done by English hands, unsurpassable when the workman chooses to do all he knows by that of any living nation.'

Sheffield was a world-class city for its practical skills, particularly metalworking. Amidst the city's poverty and genius, Freeman laid the groundwork for theatrical performances and cultural development. He was deeply inspired by Rudolf Steiner's threefold social order, and he saw new solutions for some of the old problems of poverty and unemployment. In this way he built on the work of John Ruskin, who had also championed cultural development in the region.

Ruskin built the foundations for agricultural and community development, museums and further education; a legacy to which Arnold Freeman was the ideal successor. Freeman was a warrior of simplicity and authentic, simple living. His strength stemmed from his daily practice of this lifestyle. Physical and financial limitations did not curb his vision or potential.

Under Freeman's directorship the Sheffield Educational Settlement initiative grew and flourished. During this period Freeman lectured widely and published prolifically, ensuring that Rudolf Steiner's vision for societal change and development was at the forefront of everything he did. This brought him as many challenges as successes.

As the Ruskin Mill Trust continues Freeman's work today, it honours his memory and his vision for society. The Trust is the current custodian of a long and continual effort to free human beings, to reimagine their potential.

Having planted his initiative in the poorest community in Sheffield, the Trust continued Freeman's work in the west side of Sheffield, a wealthy and privileged district. Christopher Boulton then built the Merlin Theatre adjoining Tintagel House in a transformation of the Sheffield Educational Settlement in Sheffield's poorest community. When the Merlin Theatre/ Tintagel site had reached a certain stage, it was passed on to the Ruskin Mill Trust and in part returned to the city centre.

The Trust felt a responsibility for Freeman's original intent and legacy: how are the under-privileged in Sheffield provided for? The Ruskin Mill Trust's area of expertise was working with Rudolf Steiner's methods in special needs education, whilst incorporating John Ruskin's vision and Freeman's cultural and dramatic legacy.

Freeman also had a vision for specialist care. At one point, he worked with Dr König on a possible project. This did not materialise. It is my view that the Ruskin Mill Trust picked up this untried collaboration and brought it to life by finding the right location and funding and were able to follow through with the founding of Freeman College.

In looking at the essence of Arnold Freeman's gift, it centres very much on Rudolf Steiner's spiritual science for adult education. Freeman yearned for a 'new university' predicated on spiritual science – a university of the spirit:

'*The institution needed by the present age must not aim at affecting merely the head of man, nor merely his heart. It must set itself to enrich his whole spirit with that which expressed in three words is **Beauty**, **Truth** and **Goodness**...*

We plead for a new university...'

The Ruskin Mill Trust, for many years, has been researching this quest for a new higher education facility drawing on Rudolf Steiner's spiritual science and the deep yearning of Arnold Freeman. The Trust has now found a partner institution, not in Sheffield, but in nearby

Huddersfield. The University of Huddersfield has endorsed Ruskin Mill's Seven Fields of Practice in a new Master's of Arts degree. Thus, Ruskin Mill Trust's fidelity to Arnold Freeman's vision may yet bear fruit in the future.

Aonghus Gordon, OBE
Founder and Executive Chair of the Ruskin Mill Trust

Prologue

Who was Arnold James Freeman?

In a great crisis, as the present is for me, it is a relief as well as a guide, to put down frankly what I feel. This turns vagueness into precision and sorts out the material facts from the debris. (Wednesday 22nd February 1911).

The first part of this biography of Arnold James Freeman (1886-1972) is based principally on twenty-two diaries written by him in the period 1904 to 1917. More accurately they could be described as *intimate journals* because they contain more than mere notes, dates, or appointments, for Arnold James Freeman (AJF) wrote, 'not only in order to preserve an interesting record of my feelings and aspirations, but so as to help me form my thoughts'.

The diaries vary in size; the earliest ones beginning in 1904 are very small, containing little biographical detail. Others, for example from 1910 or 1911, are quite large and contain approximately twenty-thousand words each, all written in AJF's very fine hand. The remainder of the biography is based on various sources, but mainly on the Sheffield Educational Settlement Papers that I 'discovered' when I was researching the biography of Adam Bittleston, a Christian Community priest.[1]

This eventually brought me to the Special Collections at the University of Sheffield where the papers are stored in approximately one hundred and twenty-seven boxes. Before my 'discovery' not many researchers had consulted them since John Roberts rescued them when the site at Shipton Street, the original location of the Sheffield Educational Settlement, was demolished. Roberts went on to write his Masters dissertation on the history of the Settlement but notes that by the time he rescued the archive many of the records particularly from the 1930s and 1940s had been badly damaged by rodents.[2] The documents that remain, however, are quite extensive, including correspondence, minute books, account books, some published material, play files and information about lectures, classes and activities at the Settlement. The sheer diversity of this material intrigued me and so began my research into the life of AJF. This was followed by a 2012 conference entitled 'Who Was Arnold Freeman', where I met a number of family members who subsequently loaned me the diaries.[3]

When I first started reading the diaries I was faced with a mass of detail. Some of the entries are quite striking as he visits and talks to numerous people; either family members, close friends, passing acquaintances or even strangers. He would also go to lectures, sermons and performances of plays, including reading and seeing many by Shakespeare. Some of the days appear to be so overcrowded that it is as though they last seventy-two hours rather than twenty-four. Therefore, I have had to be very selective in my choice of material and it might even be possible in the future to write an alternative biography using the entries I have deliberately left out. But that is the nature of biography writing, and indeed human memory itself; it is not volumes of disassociated, disjointed details but rather a story, a coherent narrative. Hence, the choice of presenting parts of this book thematically, especially for the earlier part of his life where I concentrate on particular aspects such as his religious development, people who influenced him, his interest in the occult and his romantic attachments.

Because of the richness of Freeman's life, and the amount of detail in the diaries, I decided to include this longer than usual prologue with the intention of offering the reader a sense for his character; his unique humour, his foibles, his fears, his hopes, his interests, his desires, his weaknesses and inconsistencies, so you already know him a little before you start reading the biography. A somewhat unusual approach, for a somewhat unusual character.

Arnold Freeman was renowned for his unconventional appearance. A colleague tells the story of Arnold in a 'sort of hiking garb, a rucksack on his back and heavy dusty boots on his feet. It could have been the outfit of

a pilgrim, and all his life he was in some sense
a pilgrim, never a settler, always a seeker for
more light'.[4] It is said he always wore a tweed
jacket and flannel trousers and on rare
occasions the trousers matched the jacket.
His taste for alternative clothing, sustained
since his Oxford days by buying only from
second-hand shops, once nearly landed him
in prison. During the Second World War,
Freeman was taken to the police station on
suspicion of being a spy, after he had been
spotted in his strange cloths and taking notes
from a German book at a train station, while
'bound for Swinton or Mexborough to give
one of his WEA lectures', and it was only after
the intervention of the Bishop of Sheffield
that he was released.[5]

*1949 photo in the News
Chronicle accompanying
article entitled 'The
Philosopher of the Dark
Streets'.*

According to contemporaries he had an equally unconventional
personality. He was sometimes described as the 'Philosopher of the Dark
Streets' because of his unique campaign against ignorance on the streets
of Sheffield. As George Bernard Shaw wrote in 1940:

> Mr Freeman is an exceptional character. Instead of devoting his very
> considerable ability to the acquisition of a comfortable fortune
> in the Sheffield Industries, he has spent his life in an attempt to
> achieve the spiritual regeneration and aesthetic cultivation of the
> inhabitants, mostly at his own expense. In short, nothing is too
> crazy for Mr Freeman. (*Sheffield Telegraph and Independent*,
> 2nd August 1940).

The Guardian described him as 'frail to the point of being diaphanous',
with a great desire to give all men and women a touch of the philosopher,
a touch of the artist, a touch of the poet, and a touch of the rebel. Indeed,
some of the Settlement's inhabitants became rebel enough to be branded
'communists' by the Guardian on Freeman's retirement. Though Freeman

was not himself a communist, the Settlement never closed its doors on those who held alternative political or religious beliefs.

Arnold James Freeman was a keen and talented sportsman. He played football, tennis and swam regularly in the nude. One June day in 1908, during his time at Oxford, an anonymous tip-off reported him for 'bathing in a state of nudity'. This was probably not the first time he had bathed naked in one of the swim holes of the river Cherwell, but this time it was brought to the attention of the police. He tells us, however, that he wrote such a cunning defence that 'they decided to take no further proceedings against me'. We will never know who reported him or what reasons he gave in his defence, but what this one short anecdote illustrates about AJF is his very persuasive way with words; in writing and speech he was eloquent, assured, and sometimes forcefully to the point.

When it comes to his faith, however, we see that this talent had its darker sides. He would often become overzealous and forceful when presenting his point of view, especially when the subject was controversial such as his views on socialism or religion. Later in life his close collaborator Charles Davy, who co-founded the Anthroposophical magazine *The Golden Blade* with him, made the observation that 'Arnold could be pugnacious, prickly, obstinate', and vehement in his expression. In his early twenties he wrote, printed and published religious tracts to propagate his own personal gospel and to serve Jesus Christ, walking around his local neighbourhood distributing his writings and wearing a sandwich board. On one occasion, following a fierce argument about the suffragette movement with the conservative Mrs Harris, he even wrote a letter to the Highbury Quadrant Magazine challenging anyone who dared to a public debate on the matter.

His combative and sometimes quarrelsome personality often caused friction in the family. For example, after attending a lecture by John Clifford he was told by his brother Peter that he should not show so much enthusiasm when trying to convince family and friends to apply themselves to his version of practical Christianity, as this had caused some of them to dismiss him as just 'young and mad.' This proved very difficult for the young Arnold who wrote of the matter:

Not to be enthusiastic! Tell me not to breathe! More imposing still, at any moment Christ may come to gather up the elect. The sluggish indifference of people just appals me.

Perhaps this obnoxious note to his character was down to his childhood experience of cold baths first thing every morning. The rumour is that all the children had to go through the daily ritual of lining up outside the bathroom and immersing themselves from head to toe in a bath of cold water as this, they were told, would prolong their lives. Anecdotal evidence tells us that Arnold continued this ritual every day for the remainder of his life as did his brother Peter. His continuance of such practices reflects his deep lifetime preoccupation with the occult and ancient wisdom, pursued in the hope that he could develop his 'supernatural powers.' For AJF, a starting point in this journey was joining the Theosophical Society, and he later became 'mesmerised' by the work of a Chicago guru named TK.

Freeman championed alternative ideological positions all his life. On his twenty-first birthday he pinned up a poster on his wall with his personal 'gospel' written on it. He identified himself as nonconformist, unorthodox, unconventional, indecent and a lunatic. The historical personages whom he revered at the time included George Fox the founder of the Quakers, William Booth the founder of the Salvation Army, Robert Louis Stevenson, George Bernard Shaw, Socrates, Diogenes, Rousseau and St. Francis. The posters he hung in his rooms in Oxford, that he referred to as his 'sort of museum for advanced thought' illustrate his views. He had one captioned '*Temptation*' of a 'green faced vegetarian looking longingly at the juicy joints of a butcher's shop'; Freeman was a lifelong vegetarian. Other posters included 'Votes for Women, notices for Free Food, Free Thought and Free Love'. There was also a photograph of the anarchist who shot the King of Portugal. While AJF would get along with people at first, they would quickly discover his 'insanity'. As he put it:

Vegetarianism, no tea, Socialism, Spiritualism, second-hand clothes, cremation, New Theology! It is the price paid for honesty.

However, Arnold Freeman's alternative views and character did not preclude him from mixing with the leading members of Edwardian Society, for his way with words likely helped win him their recognition. For instance, he had a good relationship with George Bernard Shaw and met him and his wife Charlotte regularly for lunch. In September 1910 he had dinner with Sidney and Beatrice Webb, the founders of the London School of Economics. Also present was Charles Mostyn Lloyd, a barrister, social activist, advisor to the Webbs and lecturer on social administration at the LSE, as well as Clifford Sharp, the future editor of the New Statesman and later a fierce opponent of World War One. In 1909, after he was appointed an assistant to Sidney Webb, running a joint seminar with him at the LSE Arnold reflected as follows on his social position:

> It gives me a start sometimes to think of my progress upward. Here am I who was a boy of no special aptitude for study, running a seminar with a man who, says Bernard Shaw, will be of more use to England than any other man of his time. Here I am writing a pamphlet to which Dr Clifford, the greatest nonconformist alive, writes a preface. Here I am on intimate terms with Hay Morgan, the idol of my youth, and a man who may be Prime Minister one day.

Freeman was also a great practical joker. A member of his family, for example, told me that it was not unusual for him when sitting on a train or when he was in a public place to put on a clown's nose and start playing the fool. There are many references to his tomfoolery in his diary; on one of the most interesting escapades he and his friend Marsh Roberts, tramped to France 'dressed in shabby old trousers, tattered Norfolks, old yellow Macintoshes and bandalero green hats.' On their first day they wandered around Reading begging and selling picture post cards. Striking up a conversation with two other fellows, 'Marsh enlivened the time by telling them… my name was Trotty Arnold, a clerk who had lost his job by robbing the till {and} an insatiable boozer and a thorough loose liver'. They visited several pubs where Marsh was quite well known to the barmaids. Freeman thought they found much more pity in the pubs than in the churches. They slept the night at Westies 'in a rather dirty bed' and the next morning caught the train to London still dressed in their rags and many people were 'perplexed by our gracious manner and bandit hats'.

They booked a weekend excursion, travelled via Folkestone to Boulogne and eventually arrived in Paris where they tramped about for several hours. 'Outside Cooks place we came across a guide of theirs who offered to take us to the Temple of Beauty', which turned out to be an ordinary house guarded by a woman. They entered and 'the next moment before we were aware of what was happening we were surrounded by a ring of naked girls. They were all entirely nude… the one nearest me was a girl of fourteen whom the manageress thought would just do for me'. Freeman says he was 'dumbfounded' but they took matters in hand, promised to return later that evening and quietly walked out. 'I was disgusted by the whole business. The Temple of Beauty was a temple of hideous ugliness.' His reaction to this experience, he says, was not because he was 'refined', 'I am sensual as all men are and have the sexual passion but… these ugly wretches with their painted faces disgusted me. Besides the commercialisation of the whole thing is so horrible'. He was abhorred by the lack of romance in such a relationship, 'this sort of organized sexual indulgence is deprived of all romance.'

Despite these remarks Freeman was very curious about prostitution. As we shall see later he had conversations with his friend Juliet Stuart Poyntz about female sex workers and he once visited the Leicester Lounge in London ostensibly for 'fun', but it may have been more than pure curiosity that he mentions his visit. He says that on this occasion he:

> Sat with a Spanish girl, a charming young woman. I talked to her exactly as if it was my actual intention to go with her to her flat… Marsh sat next me talking to an awfully pretty Russian girl… the head waiter came up to us to protest against us remaining there without having a drink. Marsh declared proudly that he was insulted and we walked out.

By the end of his life AJF was 'well-soaked in Shakespeare's plays'. On a visit to Stratford the mischievous fun-loving side to his character comes through when he writes that:

Everything at Stratford was soused with Shakespeare. We stayed at the Shakespeare. We went to see Shakespeare's wife's house, the Shakespeare memorial, the Shakespeare theatre, Shakespeare's school. We bought Shakespeare postcards and Shakespeare relics. We ate Shakespeare soup with Shakespeare spoons. We slept in Shakespeare beds in Shakespeare rooms and dreamt about Shakespeare.

The bold, impertinent and flirtatious Freeman is also revealed when he went with his friend Biske 'to call on Prince Kropotkin (1842-1921) at Onslow Villas'. Kropotkin was 'a celebrated anarchist', a socialist, an activist, a revolutionary and many other things, who had escaped from Russia for his activism and went into exile in 1876 in Switzerland, France and England. Freeman's intention was to ask the Prince to speak at their newly formed 'revolutionary' Fraternity of Reason at Oxford. Unfortunately the Prince was not at home but they were entertained for five minutes by his 'charming daughter', who told them that her father probably couldn't make Oxford, which prompted (flirtatious) Freeman to ask whether she could come. With a 'pretty shake of her head' she said no and continued with her mother to pack for a journey to Southern Italy.

This brings us to that side of Freeman that could be absurd and self-contradictory. We know he was a notorious clown and prankster, but why, for example, did he attend the garden party of an organisation that was deeply conservative in its outlook? The event he attended was part of a larger network of social activities organized by the Primrose League whose agenda was to promote conservative values and advance the political agenda of the Conservative party. One might imagine a sardonic grin on the socialist Freeman's face when two ladies tried to persuade him to join the League and he took with him the forms to fill out. On one occasion in 1905 he attended a debate at the Oxford Union where the proposition was: '*This House would approve of some form of National Service*'. Given his later abhorrence and opposition to military intervention and his conscientious objection during the First World War it is surprising to see him making the following statement:

Wyatt, secretary of the National Service League, made a spirited speech in favour of it. He suggested compulsory drill and rifle practice at schools... I am inclined to agree that this would be advised if India or England were ever seriously menaced, we should make a sorry show against the enemy.

In 1908 his mother accused him of changing his religion from one day to the next. From one perspective, and from the evidence in the diaries, she was to a certain extent correct. He delved deeply into Christian Science, although he thought that they relied too much on the founder Mary Baker Eddy. Quite often he declared himself an agnostic but later he pronounced himself a believer in the New Theology. A visit to the Reverend Vincent Stuckey Stratton Coles (1845-1929), principal of Pusey House, offers another example of AJF's fluctuating approach to religious questions. Coles' theological beliefs were at the other end of the 'theological spectrum' from Freeman's who at this time identified himself as a staunch non-conformist. Freeman left Coles with a fairer appreciation for the Catholic religion, although he said he would always remain a dissenter.

Freeman, it might be correct to say, was desperate to get into a good university and a little more desperate to get into Oxford. This seems, however, somewhat of a paradox because when his friend Marsh Roberts experienced a period of heavy drinking Freeman made one of his many passionate and verbal onslaughts against the privileged system of private education and Oxford University, blaming these for Roberts' downfall:

Not a friend has stretched out a helping hand to him. This is all that this accursed Public School and University system has done for him! For most men it means complete ruin... all they learn is to look upon life as a pleasure ground as a huge bauble made for their amusement... in this city the characters of hundreds are under-mined every year... if the devil has one spot on earth which he regards with especial favour, I'd say it was Oxford.

AJF was born into a society where the inequalities of *wealth and poverty were* starkly delineated and wealth and power was concentrated into a few hands. The investigations conducted by Booth in London and Rowntree in

York, both found that poverty, especially in the urban areas, was wide-spread.[6] Freeman spent the first twenty-five years of his life living and working in Edwardian London. Even when he was at Oxford, he maintained close contact with his family and friends and visited them at regular intervals in and out of term time, so he was acutely aware of the social problems which, from evidence in the diaries, he witnessed on a regular basis. One incident he writes about is when he attended the magistrate court whilst on a one-week placement reporting for the North London Guardian:

> I realised vividly that there is a dark side to life which we in our comfort and blindness rarely see. Those poor fellows, drunk and disorderly and what not; were they more deserving of punishment than the bloated old magistrate who sentenced them to 10 shillings or 7 days or to two months hard labour?

This period was also one of population growth, especially in London. The 1911-census report shows that the number of people residing in London grew substantially between 1901 and 1911. The population of Greater London rose from 6,581,402 people in 1901 to 7,251,358 people in 1911, an overall increase of 10.2%. The London underground had grown and cars began to replace the horse drawn carriage on the road.[7] Freeman tells us that he 'got excited' on a journey to Stratford on Avon travelling with friends in an exclusive Dutch built Spyker reaching at one point a speed of 55mph. Another time on his way to Letchworth he took a lift with Felice Nazzaro (1881-1940) an Italian racing driver who had just set the world speed record at 127mph. Freeman says he had a wonderful devil-may-care attitude and 'we went over 60 miles an hour at times.' By 1914 Britain had around 400,000 licensed vehicles on the road.

There were also major shifts in the political landscape of the country when the general election of 1906 brought about a remarkable transformation in Britain with the Liberals winning the election in the first 'landslide' victory of the 20th century. The dominance of the Conservative and Unionist parties ended and Freeman eventually began to fight, in various ways, for the much-needed social reform when in 1909 he began working for Sidney and Beatrice Webb.

One of the final entries in his diaries encapsulates his attitude towards life, work, love and relationships when he says: 'Doing fine work and doing it as well as I can is the very best way of becoming fine myself.' Then quoting H G Wells he writes:

Find out what you want to do, make sure that's it, and then do it with all your might, that's the way to increase one's intellect and one's soul. Not introspection but noble service.[8]

Chapter One

Early Influences

The Freeman Family

Freeman wrote comparatively little about his family, but when he did, he invariably spoke in positive terms. Their occasional differences in opinion were soon resolved, and on the whole his relationship with his mother, father, brothers and sisters was harmonious. In a short entry in the diary, he describes his mother and father as follows:

> To all of us nine children, she has been goodness itself, a completely selfless person. My father… like my mother he lived in and for all of us children; he helped us in every possible way with our sports and our studies and was never content unless we 'got first' and 'got top'; carrying his hatred of respectability and conventionality and affectation to the most disconcerting lengths, he was genuine through and through; highly cultured though he was for a man of business; he dropped his h's in order to get on better with his work people.

On the day of his father's death Freeman wrote that 'he loved and admired him not because he was his father but he was a grand man.' AJF was grateful that he had stood for his father's ideals of being 'true to oneself and caring nothing for the opinion of the world… for what is good in me he is more than any other person responsible'. His father 'cared nothing for the churches or the creeds… he let us go our own road'. It was his father who was instrumental in persuading him to apply for the University of Oxford and both parents visited him at regular intervals when he was studying there. Although his relationship with his mother was at times tense, she was certainly a role model in her honesty, tenacity and untiring commitment to the family and the business.

Born into a relatively 'well off' non-conformist family, his father, George James Freeman (1853-1908) inherited a 'segar' factory in Hoxton from his father James Reykers Freeman, who had been sent to Holland as a young man to learn the cigar business. On his return, he opened a shop in Shoreditch in 1839 and was probably the first person to manufacture cigars in Britain, under the business name of J.R. Freeman and Son. The shop was expanded into a factory with a further extension being built in Cardiff in 1908.

In 1875, Freeman's father, George, married Edith Marion Henderson, the daughter of a Baptist minister. Together they had six sons and three daughters: Donald George (1877-1937) followed his father into the cigar business and eventually took over its management. Ralph (1880-1950) became a civil engineer and helped design the Sydney Harbour Bridge. Then there were Arnold (1886-1972), Peter (1888-1956) who ran the cigar business in Penarth and later became an MP, Frank (1890-1953), who also became a bridge designer, and Edward (1878-1946), sometimes referred to as Ted, who was an electrician in the company of Tyler and Freeman, Chancery Lane, London. Then there were the Freeman sisters: Edith Elizabeth Freeman (1884-1946), also known as Elsie, who married James Edmondson, 1st Baron Sandford who was Conservative MP for Banbury from 1922 to 1945. Ada Marion Freeman (1894-1975) married Charles Brandon Dansie (1896-1973) in 1922, was known in the family as Daisy, became a doctor and was, for a short time, George Bernard Shaw's medical consultant. Ellen Dorothy Freeman (1894-1986), known in the family as Dolly, was Daisy's twin. She was a talented artist and never married.

With such a large family, even by the standards of the time, Arnold's childhood was not always easy, especially when family members were ill. Mike Bloxham, who had access to the 'Black-Books'; the Freeman family journal, relates the story of one particularly challenging year.[9] From 1894 to 1895, nearly the whole family was ill. Arnold and two of his sisters had scarlet fever, his father had typhoid and six others had measles. Only Arnold's mother and brother Donald were spared.

During this 'dreadful year' his mother carried the full responsibility for the business and for nursing everyone back to health. She wrote the following in the aftermath of the crisis:

> We finally decided to leave Hoxton… and every morning when the nurse came on duty, I went out house hunting… I used to spend the days going about, get to bed at about 5 o'clock in the afternoon and was up again at 10 o'clock to take on the night duty.

The whole family had been living in premises above the factory and it was due to their mother's hard work that more spacious accommodation was found at 6, Woodberry Down, just across the road from Finsbury Park. The property included a tennis court and a field in which they were obliged to keep a flock of black sheep, and all for the price of £600.

Theirs was a fun-loving family, with AJF continually 'playing the fool', but also with a wealth of 'cultural activity' such as reading and acting in plays, playing charades, card games, reciting and singing. Faith also played an important part in their lives, especially Arnold's, as can be seen in his promotion of 'active Christianity' within the family. Along with his cousin Lawrence, AJF established a Society for Active Christians, which they were constantly persuading family and friends to join. In addition to this, they met regularly in their own Christian Endeavour group, reading and studying the bible and giving their own sermons. After a Boxing Day spent with the family, Arnold commented on the differences and similarities between the six Freeman brothers:

> We six brothers all do admire one another and stand in a curious sort of isolated conjoined attitude to each other… we are a curious lot. Each with a strong individuality, each with different religious and political ideas and yet all uniting in a sort of practical religious outlook on life that brings us far nearer to one another than any two average men of any political party.

Early Education and Role Models

All six boys attended Haberdasher Aske's School, originally located in Hoxton but later in 1903 moving to Westbere Road in Hampstead. All three girls, as far as can be ascertained, were privately educated and possibly at some point attended the North London Collegiate School.

Arnold started at the school in 1893.[10] The school magazine, The Skylark, reported that the Haberdasher School Scholarship awarded a Senior Scholarship to Arnold J. Freeman (The Bicentenary Scholarship, instituted in 1892 for boys who reached the sixth form after entering school in the first). After ten years at the school, Freeman received praise in The Skylark for being among the best in football, swimming and athletics, as well as academic studies. He was loyal to the school and a good influence, which is probably best demonstrated by his captaincy of the football team. It was reported that he distinguished himself by his perseverance and his devotion to the interests of the team; 'no team could wish for a better captain'. From 1903 Freeman, along with Noel Mabbs, was editor of the school magazine. He was also known for his love of entertaining and making the best of any situation. Money, clothes and comfort meant little to him, which was just as well for a schoolboy in Edwardian England.

As a teenager Freeman read a lot of Charles Dickens and at one point in early February 1904, he resolved to adopt the attitude of Martin Tapley from the book Martin Chuzzlewit, who was always jolly. Tapley became a role model for Freeman, who reasoned in his diaries that 'to be always cheerful is a splendid characteristic and I am going to try and be a Tapley'. His interest in leading a good life likely led to his being given, on his eighteenth birthday, a copy of John Lubbock's *The Use of Life*, a nineteenth century 'lifestyle' or 'self-help' manual which was much criticised by John Ruskin but which was a best-seller.

AJF's early influences were not just literary, and the preachers Reginald John Campbell (1867-1956) and John Clifford (1836-1923) were significant role models to him at this stage in his life. Campbell was a Congregationalist minister and proponent of the New Theology who, after a period in Brighton, preached at the City Temple in Holborn about a twenty-minute cycle ride from AJF's home. In 1907 Freeman attended one of Campbell's lectures and found that Campbell reminded him of Christ 'more than do most of his opponents... His great aim is to spiritualise the social movement. If he can do that let him preach as much New Theology as he likes!' On another occasion he spoke to Campbell after a service and was struck by his 'wonderful personality... expressed especially in his honest grip and in his eyes that seem to look right through you.' Campbell advised him that Mansfield College in Oxford would be a good theological college to apply to but warned the young Freeman to 'do (his) own thinking' while at university; a message that would remain with him during his Oxford years.

On another visit in June 1908, AJF was again captivated by Campbell's charisma and said he 'would like to have kissed him... he smiles so beautifully and has exquisite features'. They also discussed spiritualism and automatic writing, a phenomenon Campbell 'believed to be perfectly genuine.' Campbell's political views would also have appealed to Freeman, especially his belief that Socialism was the practical form of Christianity and politics was the application of Christian principles to common life. Campbell was also seen as the founder of the New Theology, which holds that the divine encompasses or is manifested in the material world, or as Campbell put it, 'New Theology is but the religious articulation of the social movement.'

Freeman did not necessarily agree with all that Campbell believed, in fact he said that after reading his book *The New Theology* he thought of him as more of a preacher rather than a philosopher. However, what was fundamental to Campbell's religious and philosophical thought was a humanitarian vision of a socialist movement working towards the establishment of the Kingdom of God on earth. This was an ideal that Freeman took deeply to heart for the remainder of his life.

Campbell also worked with John Clifford another 'role model' within AJF's circle at this time. Both were supporters of the Liberal party's political and social agenda which included, among other things, the values and beliefs of individual liberty, and an abhorrence of the privileged position of the Anglican Church in the education system.

Before Freeman formally met him, John Clifford had attained not only high status as a leader among the English Baptist community, but also international recognition. For instance, he had served as the president of the Baptist World Alliance in 1905 when it met in London. Clifford was fully involved in the political issues of the day, championing the cause of the working classes, which would have endeared him to Freeman. He campaigned against the Boer War, the Education Act of 1902, the House of Lords, slavery in the Congo, and militarism, and promoted temperance, and land reform, reflecting traditional Nonconformist and radical concerns. He also became a national figure in the passive resistance movement, whose members refused to pay education rates, arguing that they infringed on freedom of conscience.

Freeman may well have read Clifford's article in the *Primitive Methodist* published on December 14th, 1905, in the wake of Prime Minister Balfour's resignation, in which he condemned the government and called for an immediate general election:

> The last two Elections pronounced a wholesale condemnation on the most exalted ideals of human life, ideals for which our fathers fought and suffered and died, and ideals which are still to us the very breath of life – such as liberty of conscience, the freedom of religion from State control; national sobriety, and the equalizing of opportunity for all citizens alike. The penalties of that fatal mistake are all around us and upon us.

Clifford saw politics as an extension of religion. Writing in the General Baptist Magazine he said: 'To a Christian man, politics are part of the Kingdom of God and should be dealt with in the same spirit of earnestness and zeal for right and goodness and humanity with which he advocates missions or works in the Sunday School'. The issue which concerned Clifford the most was education. The focus of his attack was the privileged position of the Anglican and Roman Catholic schools in a state-supported system of elementary education. One might call Clifford a Christian Socialist as he recognised the intimate relationship between Christianity and the social question. In his view, Churches should become organisations

for the social welfare of the people. He opposed the Roman Catholic and
Anglican Churches because they established the priest as the sole inter-
preter of the Christian faith. He feared that creeds could become tools of
'theological tyranny' which could be used as instruments of coercion upon
individual consciences. He believed drink was at the heart of the nation's
social problems; demoralising the working population and leading to
debauchery, crime, and brutality.

One evening in 1905, after taking Communion, Freeman had his
first personal meeting with Clifford, having attended many of his lectures
and sermons over the past two years:

> At last he came along and I said I should like to speak to him.
> So he took me into his vestry and I sat down near him at the table.
> His kind old face fairly beamed when I told him about Grandpa
> and he said 'Give my love to him'… then I said boldly, 'How can I
> be a preacher like you?'

Clifford replied by telling him it takes a long time, and that he always
kept a book on preaching with him, 'because he was afraid of becoming
conservative'. Freeman told him that he was going to Oxford to study
history and Clifford suggested that this was a splendid training for the
ministry. They conversed further on passive resistance and the politician
Hay Morgan whom Freeman held in high esteem.

1904-5, and Preparations for University

Freeman began the year 1904 with a trip in April up to Grangemouth in
Scotland. This was his first trip by sea, and consequently his first experience of sea sickness:

> When they handed me the basin I tried to put a pleasant face on…
> the ship was playing pitch and toss with the breakers and for a few
> moments I lay pensive in bed, then the horrible truth rushed upon
> me and I leapt out of bed, was violently knocked backwards… and
> staggered into a cabin close at hand where there were basins for the
> needy. I took a little brandy – what awful stuff but it was too late.

He was sick a few more times in different parts of the ship and on arrival wryly congratulated himself for not paying the nine and sixpence for meals beforehand! After sending postcards to family, Freeman, for the first time in his life set foot on land 'that was not that of my native land'. He continued his journey to Glasgow by train to visit his cousin Rea, who was working there, but both boys ended up with scarlet fever and spent six weeks in hospital.

In mid- to late-Victorian England scarlet fever reached epidemic proportions but by the beginning of the twentieth century, probably due to better nutrition, improved sanitation and stricter legislation, death rates began to fall. The Infectious Diseases (Notification) Act of 1889 made it compulsory for patients with infectious diseases to enter isolation in hospital, and so AJF, having contracted scarlet fever for the second time, had to do just that.[11]

He describes how at first his cousin Rea was ill and how, because of his own sore throat and swollen glands, he had visited the doctor who gave him some medicine. Later, the doctor made a house visit, together with a hospital doctor and diagnosed scarlet fever. An ambulance was organized, books and writing materials gathered together and the 'van' arrived to take them away. They arrived at the isolation hospital, where their hair was cut, they were bathed and put to bed. This caused Freeman to reflect on his previous bout of scarlet fever when he was just eight years old. He recounts in the diaries how he remembered playing Halma with his mother; 'punching a nurse in the nose when having a bath' and having 'visions of a Scrap Album, painting books, kindergarten and a Round Robin'.

Freeman didn't go into great detail about the treatment he received in Glasgow, but he did note that every four hours, day and night, he was required to gargle, had his mouth steamed and his temperature, pulse and breath measured. As for the food:

> We fed on milk and barley and Imperial (a mixture of lemons, Cream of Tartar and some other things), designed to clear the blood, lower the temperature and throw less work on the kidneys.

At one point he got a fish bone lodged in his throat which didn't help his condition as his glands were getting worse and the fish bone made them bleed a little. He became very frustrated when the doctor took so long to examine him, only to ask that he come back later to have the fish bone removed.

So much for that start to his year, but by June Freeman was back in London, fully recovered, and joyful that his 'confinement in a prison' was over. He travelled by train and on arrival was met by his father at St Pancras who drove him home in the trap. A long weekend was spent in Frinton with his mother, and he returned to school on Wednesday.

In July 1904, Freeman took a significant step towards his educational future, with a visit to University College London to talk to Professor Montague about UCL's School of History and to ask 'Professor Pollard whether he would coach me'. Francis Charles Montague (1858-1935) was professor emeritus at UCL and lectured in modern history at Oriel College Oxford. Albert Frederick Pollard (1869-1948) held the part-time chair in Constitutional History at UCL and spent the rest of his time coaching students. Freeman was keen to study in London, but he was later discouraged by Mr Hinton, his tutor at school, and by his father, both of whom encouraged him to apply for Oxford.

July 1904 was an important month for AJF from a religious perspective as well, what with his brother Ralph and sister Elsie being 'received into the church', when they took their first communion, and his final day at school was Wednesday July 28th. Although Arnold wrote that this was 'the most memorable day in my life up to the present', he was very saddened and compared it to 'the feeling of losing a dear friend. I have left school and I cannot realise it… my school days are over – I have not yet realised what that means.'

The August holidays were filled with various pursuits with his extended family, including visits to uncles and aunts and other relatives normally resulting in an outing with his cousins, especially Rea and Lawrence. His days were full of activities, he described, for example, how one day they rose at six in the morning, proceeded to Finsbury Park, took a boat on the lake and fooled around with others by pushing them 'back and forward'. Then it was off to breakfast at No. 6 with loud singing in the drawing room and grandpa throwing them out because it sounded 'like a tavern'. They played cricket, had dinner at No. 13, read some Shakespeare, told stories in the garden and then went to 'Auntie's school and sang to the rafters and returned home to have tea'. The day finished with games in the garden, then off to bed.

The academic year 1904-1905 was dominated by preparation for his school's final examination and the entrance exams for the various Oxford colleges he applied for. AJF studied assiduously, sometimes for hours on end, and visited a private history tutor in the hope that it might help him gain a scholarship. On Tuesday 6th December he sat an entrance examination with papers on Chivalry, the medieval period, and general knowledge. This was followed by an interview, which was then referred to as a viva voce examination. Afterwards he vividly described the experience in his diary:

> I went through a big door at the end of the hall and down a winding flight of gloomy steps and was ushered into a room where sat, I think seven examiners. Some of them seemed to be taking notes of the honey that flowed from my lips and two of then plied me with questions.

After Oxford he travelled down to Cardiff and later Penarth to meet his father and on the evening of December 11th AJF and his father watched the Benson Company perform Hamlet. Freeman was 'not favourably impressed' with Frank Benson or his 'impersonation of Hamlet', despite his being one of the leading Shakespearean actors of the day. The next day was Sunday and after a swim in the freezing cold sea he went to a service in Pontypridd with a friend and a 'minister' who, he tells us, gave him some good hints 'for the ministerial profession'.

The whole point of this trip to Wales, however, was for AJF to experience a Welsh Revival meeting, some of which took place in the Baptist Chapel at Maerdy. On their arrival, they had hardly entered the Chapel 'before someone in the congregation began a hymn and at once everyone joined in. The effect was magnificent.' Freeman was really impressed with the Welsh voices, saying he had never 'heard singing to compare with what

I have heard today'. For two hours they stood in the Chapel and listened to 'all kinds of speaking, praying and singing.' At about twelve noon Evan Roberts, the leader of the movement, 'entered with a small retinue.' After speaking for about half an hour in Welsh, Roberts asked the congregation to stand up and say they loved the Lord Jesus Christ, which elicited an amazing response for all those present: 'Everybody as far as I could see… stood up and said that they loved God. It was a wonderful sight; more wonderful in this century of matter of fact.'

Evan Roberts was one of the central figures in the Welsh Revival who, it was said, filled the churches to capacity with his inspired preaching. It is alleged that within a couple of months Wales was a changed nation. Crime was reduced to almost nothing. Often magistrates were given a ceremonial pair of white gloves when they arrived at the courtroom, signifying that there were no cases to try. The Times reported that 'the whole population had been suddenly stirred by a common impulse. Religion had become the absorbing interest of their lives'. Freeman writes that everything was so spontaneous, 'everything was unprepared and passionate', with people breaking out in torrents of prayer and repentance. During that day he had the opportunity to shake hands with Roberts and he also observed the entrance of Gypsy Smith another leading evangelist of the time.[12]

On his return to Penarth, AJF asked his father if he would like to have his help in running the family cigar business as his father had 'been down lately', but he received a definite 'No!' much to his private relief; 'I shudder at the thought of a business life'. Attendance at the Revival had obviously made a deep impression on Freeman and almost certainly consolidated his decision to train for the ministry.

After Penarth it was another visit to Oxford to sit the exam for Lincoln College and Freeman reflected, with some justification, that he would have done much better if he had concentrated on English History. Instead, he had to tackle questions such as: *The Ten Commandments Do Not Apply to International Relations* or *The Great Poet Stands Aloof from the Politics of his Time.* He chose the latter question but found out later that he had not been selected and his applications for Balliol College and New College were also unsuccessful. In January 1905 he sat the examinations for Merton College.

Christmas 1904 and the New Year 1905 were spent at home in London with the extended family. His diaries mention Grandma Henderson's illness and her death in January 1905. There are also references to his older sister Elsie's deteriorating mental health which continued over a number of years, causing problems with her later marriage to Edmondson. Evidence in the diaries suggests that Elsie may have suffered from some sort of manic depression, as AJF observed that some days she was suicidal and on others she was very cheerful.

On February 15th Freeman declared that his educational fate was 'decided once and for all'. His school tutor Mr Horton had promised to recommend to the governors that an award of £50.00 per annum be given to Freeman to support his studies in Oxford, which motivated him to begin work on his entrance examination to Christchurch.

In March 1905 he visited the Law Courts realising 'what an ordeal it must be for anyone who had had no practice in argument or public speaking… it is worthwhile learning to speak'. This visit offered AJF further motivation to learn 'to become a practised speaker… I regularly start a debate every morning at breakfast and usually at tea. I argue whenever I have the opportunity'. Such practice was for him a good mental training as was memorising and reading poetry out loud.

Part of his 'training' also involved attending lectures, sermons and addresses. For example, he went to the events of the Ethical Society at Southplace Chapel in Finsbury, where they sang a hymn, heard two solos by a girl, heard a reading of Spedding's Discourses followed by an address on Francis Bacon (1561-1626). AJF was not satisfied with the address on Bacon, thinking that the lecturer's comments about Bacon were not only wrong but unjust. A week later he attended a lecture at the Ethical Society on St. Francis of Assisi followed by another on the same subject at the Positivist Society where he was invited to a meeting of the Franciscan Society which, due to other commitments, he was unable to attend.

The first six months of 1905 were spent mostly working hard in preparation for his school matriculation examination and his scholarship examinations for Christchurch in June and St Johns in July. He was also practising his preaching by reading his sermons to Grandpa Henderson and asking John Clifford for advice on speaking techniques. This was supplemented by taking elocution lessons with a tutor at the polytechnic.

After these exams, in August, he was able to relax a little with two weeks' camping on Hayling Island, organized by his school, and punctuated by visits to Portsmouth to take Lawrence's Sunday School class. This was followed by a visit to Buxton in the Peak District for a few days to care for a Mr Russell who was convalescing at the Spa for his rheumatism. Freeman was later joined by his brother Ralph and they went on expeditions to different landmarks including the Cat and Fiddle, the highest pub in England. Back in London he spent time with the family and went on a short trip to Arundel with his cousin Lawrence.

Then at long last, he said goodbye to his relatives at No. 13 and his grandfather gave him an inspirational picture of the Baptist preacher Charles Spurgeon (1834-1892). In the evening he went with Elsie to the Garrick Theatre to see *The Merchant of Venice*, and the following morning he rose early. His brothers gave him presents and saw him off at Kings Cross from where he travelled to Leighton to say goodbye to his friends, who presented him with a copy of Thomas à Kempis's *Imitation of Christ*. Meanwhile, Sidney Ball (1857-1918) had been trying to reach him, thinking he would be late for the matriculation ceremony, so on arrival in Oxford he contacted Ball and eventually filled out all the necessary paperwork.[13] And so it was that Arnold Freeman navigated that decisive day, and that decisive year 'between London and Oxford, School and University, Boyhood and Manhood, Home and the World.'

Chapter Two

Oxford

Oxford, Politics and Faith

Arnold James Freeman was matriculated as a member of St John's College Oxford on Friday 13th October 1905. He had gained an exhibition of £60 per year to the College, to which his school's governors added a leaving Exhibition of £50 per year for three years. On the day of his matriculation, he borrowed a cap and gown from a local tailor and bought a white tie. He thought the Latin ceremony to be 'hateful to mortals' and 'by the Gods abhorred', which is probably an early indication of his later hostile attitude towards Oxford and higher education more generally.

He entered the university with an ambitious ten-year plan for his future. His main priority was to complete his undergraduate degree in History and, as he was still enthused by the idea of becoming a preacher, he envisioned post-graduate divinity training at Mansfield College, followed by a qualification in Law, some business experience, and the opportunity to live 'among all classes of people'. His plan concluded, by the time of his thirtieth birthday, with him having his own church, and his own unique religion, or alternatively becoming 'an itinerant preacher'.

Clearly, he had very high expectations of himself and with his typical overconfident optimism he considered life at Oxford to be 'a very tame matter… best described as an ordinary life covered with a film of gold.' His views were soon changed, however, when he began to encounter the realities of student life. Coming from a social background which emphasised frugality, temperance, family values and above all hard work, he was horrified at the behaviour he witnessed, for example seeing first year students in varying states of inebriation. 'Drunkenness is universally prevalent', he remarked, and described many of his fellow students as 'rich and idle, who coming out of the restraints of public school, university freedom lets the devil make a kingdom of their hearts… the lazy brutes who do no work, swear and drink, and afterwards are given comfortable parsonages to have the spiritual care of thousands. God forgive them.'

Other horrors confronted him during Freshers' week, when he tells us that some students lit a tremendous bonfire in the middle of the quad; tearing all the doors and seats off the lavatories and throwing them on the fire. During that evening they 'de-bagged one poor nervous chap… with his thin white legs in pants as he sat on the ground in the light of this roaring fire. How long are these relics of barbarism to continue?' Equally disdainful to him was the fact that 'three or four dons' in the College were also clerics. 'I suppose', he wrote with irony, 'they can reconcile drunken-ness with their creed.'

Much of Freeman's time in Oxford was invariably preoccupied with study, but on reading the diaries one wonders how he managed to fit in all the other activities he took upon himself, including holding prayer meetings at Jericho with his friend Marsh Roberts, taking his Sunday School classes, organising and attending meetings for his Society of Active Christians or Christian Endeavour, long walks with friends where the subjects discussed ranged from politics and religion to personal magnetism and hypnotism, regular meetings with ministers from a range of denominations, generally fooling around or going on boat trips on the river, mostly with young women. He also noted the numerous religious questions he wished to address when his three-year 'imprisonment' at Oxford was over, and he didn't have to sit any more exams. 'I long to be free from examination work so that I can begin to prepare myself truly for Christ's work.'

Freeman's diaries give the impression that in his first eighteen months at Oxford he was totally absorbed in his religion; his whole life was focused on his dedication to the work of serving God and this mani-fested itself in, among other things, his distribution of tracts and pamphlets. It was not unusual for him to go into pubs to give out pieces of his own writing. One entry reads: 'I went into the public bar with bright lights and the clink of glasses and the smoke and chatter. I ordered lemonade, drank it and then gave each of the six men there a tract. I came out simply swelling with happiness; not able to help laughing aloud for joy, for Jesus had filled my heart.' Indeed, by 1906, his religious interests began to take precedence over his academic work. 'I am getting on well with my Political Science and Political Economy – almost ad nauseam, but I do not find any interest in them outside office hours; all my spare thoughts drift instinctively to religion.'

George Hay Morgan and the 1906 Election Campaign

In a period of political activity between January and February 1906, Freeman was involved with the preacher and later Liberal politician George Hay Morgan (1866-1931) with whom he had already developed a close friendship. In one of the first entries referring to Hay Morgan in 1905 he wrote: 'I am very glad to have established an intimacy with such a man, his examples, his principles and his friendship will be a strong assistance to me in my career.' AJF went to many of his sermons, sometimes attending two in one day. He was curious about Hay Morgan's success as a preacher, attributing this to the man's 'broad-minded' views and his preaching of 'sermons for life' that were 'practical and useful.' On one occasion in Cornwall where Hay Morgan was addressing over a thousand people, AJF tells us that 'Mr Morgan made a wonderful speech', which was 'more or less extempore'. What appealed to Freeman was his manner as a preacher, 'with his hands in his jacket', speaking in a 'quite colloquial way'. Much like he was 'talking to his friends at the fireside… he simply carried the audience away… I shall be nearly satisfied when I can speak like that.'

In 1906 George Hay Morgan was elected Liberal MP for Truro in Cornwall in the Liberal landslide of that year, replacing the Liberal Unionist MP Edwin Durning-Lawrence. Between 1906 and 1911 Freeman visited Truro frequently and canvassed vigorously on his friend's behalf. On one such trip to Truro, while canvassing for the 1906 election, Freeman stayed with the Polkinhorn family who were well known throughout Cornwall for their joint business ventures with Hosken and Trevithick (HTP).

This trio ran a number of businesses including flour milling, biscuit making, shipping and car dealerships, and owned various properties in the town. The Polkinhorns lived in Princes House, where Freeman stayed during his visit. He wrote of the family, 'they are friends of uncle William and on his request and at my suggestion they have invited me to stay here. They are exceedingly kind people and rabid Liberals... Mr Polkinhorn is very rich... he is also a JP (Justice of the Peace). It is a pleasure to find such an ardent radical and nonconformist.'

In the days following his arrival, Freeman travelled to some of the local villages, especially Portleven and Helston, where he gave lectures and distributed pamphlets to the local fishermen. One of the major issues in the fishing communities in Cornwall was that Irish Home Rule would exclude them from Irish waters. In a letter to a local newspaper he commented on the issue of 'Home Rule' for Ireland, which was a controversial and sensitive problem for the Liberals who had failed to deal with the problem. During the 1906 election campaign and in the following 1910 General Election the Liberals, to a certain extent, ignored this matter, concentrating more on free trade and the Chinese labour issue in South Africa. It is in this context that we read Freeman's angry response to Hay Morgan's political opponent, Sir Edwin Durning-Lawrence, who asserted in a debate that the election would be won exclusively on Home Rule. In his letter to the Western Daily Mercury of January 12th Freeman asks:

> Can any of your readers enlighten me on the following points? If a red herring and a half costs three half-pence how long will it take Sir Edwin Durning-Lawrence to discover that Cornishmen can't be bamboozled by Home Rule? Does Sir Edwin think that a tax on red herrings would lead to vice and immorality? Is it anything to do with his sufferings under *Petticoat Government* that makes Sir Edwin think so much of Home Rule? If Sir Edwin is so fond of Red Herrings, why did he vote against compensation for seamen? Is there any foundation for the rumour that the government have tried to silence Sir Edwin's dangerous opposition by offering the title of Baron of Yarmouth?

Truro had always been a relatively safe seat for the Unionist party, which made Sir Edwin's subsequent defeat by a majority of 500 all the more surprising. Some suggest that one of the reasons for Hay Morgan's victory was that he was able to attract the Methodist vote by preaching in the constituency's principal chapels. AJF helped win this vote by giving sermons in local churches, which were among the first he ever gave. His hard work was recognised in a short report in the Quadrant magazine stating that the editor had received a pamphlet from Freeman entitled *The Star of Cornwall*, with a preface written by John Clifford. It reads:

> Mr Freeman undertook a fortnight's strenuous work in this cause and sets forth in graphic language the hard-fought battle so deservedly won… their election campaign seems to have been fought on the great issues of national righteousness.

Literature and Faith

After this brief political interlude Freeman continued his spiritual progress, and as an avid reader, books played a major role in the development of his religious life. AJF often referred to the books he read in his diaries, and during this period in his life certain works and authors were clearly influential in shaping his faith. Charles Monroe Sheldon's best-selling religious fiction novel *In His Steps*, is an example of one such book. Sheldon (1857-1946) was an American Congregationalist minister, and the novel would have appealed to Freeman with its theme of moral choices in the face of poverty and deprivation. He said of the novel:

> Since reading *In His Steps* I believe more firmly than ever the necessity of actually working for God – not merely living morally…
> I should be happy if I could write a book that would do as much good as that one must be doing.

More significant for him still was Henry Drummond's (1851-1897) book, *Natural Law in the Spiritual World* published in 1883, which explores how the world of religion and spirituality relates to the physical world. Drummond argued that the disconnect between the spiritual and the physical was entirely illusory, and that faith was by no means in conflict with science. Written just a few decades after Darwin's *On the Origin of Species*, Drummond's reconciliation of the theory of evolution with God's purposes ranks among the most important and influential books concerning Christian faith and scientific progress. When published the book sold nearly half a million copies in the first year. The work facilitated a shift in AJF's thinking:

> Drummond's grand conception of Law in everything and his appli-
> cation of the scientific method to everything must be constantly
> borne in mind. I must become far more a scientist: inquiring into
> and criticising all things and always dissatisfied. I have read
> Drummond's *Natural Law in the Spiritual World* and I suppose it
> has affected me as it does most. It has made me long to know more
> science; it will further that implicit confidence which I have begun
> to feel that one day I shall actually experience Christ dwelling in me
> and do enormous work for him.

One of Freeman's friends then gave him Drummond's The Greatest Thing in the World, which is based on 1 Corinthians 13 and encourages readers to practice the power and blessing of love in every area of life. Freeman found that it 'stirred me more than any other I have ever read. Here and now, I declare my intention to try to live in accordance with the teaching in that essay. Patience; kindness; generosity; humility; courtesy; unselfish-ness; good temper; guilelessness; sincerity – these make up the supreme gift, the stature of the perfect man. I have learned from Drummond's beautiful work that the secret of personal influence is Love'.

Another book that made a deep impression on AJF was Charles Paul Marie Sabatier's biography of *Francis of Assisi* (1895). The book awakened in the twenty-one-year-old Arnold a sense of mission and a deep devotion to fulfil it. This emotional commitment to serve a higher purpose remained with him for the rest of his life. Sabatier's book became hugely popular and was translated into English within a year of publica-tion and went into some forty-five editions in a score of languages. The Catholic Church also placed it on the Index of Forbidden Books as it significantly challenged the traditional Catholic hagiographies that presented Francis as a submissive servant of the Roman Church. Sabatier (1858-1928) depicts Francis as the romantic hero pursuing the apostolic ideals of poverty and frugality, whose very existence signalled the end of the dogmatism and authority of the Catholic Church. He questioned received interpretations and associated Francis with the common people and the possibility of social reform and a religion of action. According to Sabatier, true Christianity was a religion of love, action and doctrine, ritual and institutions were corrupt and faith was something to be lived. It is therefore not surprising to find the following long reflection in Freeman's diary in March 1907 after reading the book:

> I feel that God has spoken to me again. Is it not a fact that for years deep down in my heart my great longing has been to serve Him? Is it not a fact that due to ill-health… I have failed (apparently) in almost everything I have undertaken up here. My old idol of self-worship – a gentleman triumphant alike in sports and study – lies shattered – thank God! For a truer object of devotion has taken its place. I am not sure of all it features yet, but I can perceive its outline. A life of much prayer and unconquerable love; a life of poverty and self-renunciation; a life not of political agitation or theological disputation, but of simple soul saving; a life as near to Christ's in all details as he is pleased to allow. I am not built for theology or politics; I can make no conquest by eloquence or learning; only by love and faith can I overcome the world.

The book caused Freeman to envision a life of 'abstinence, constant meditation and prayer' as his only possibility, and it brought him conclusively to the realisation that 'my work is to give people religion'.

As far as he could see the only serious problem preventing him from achieving this ascetic life of self-denial was his sore throat, as it would interfere with his chances of becoming a preacher. But this also had its positive side. At the end of 1905 Freeman reflected that his sore throat 'has perhaps been a kind of turning point in my life… by forcing me to solitary thought, it has forced me to think… I have much more vividly realised

the not to be exaggerated importance of thought.' His reading of Thomas
Corwin Horton's (1848-1932) *The Word of God* impressed on him the
utmost importance of developing his thinking over and above 'the super-
ficial training of the history school'. Studying at Oxford became for
Freeman a means to an end, 'I will not be bound by its requirements'.
He intended to work consistently on 'a severe mental training', which he
hoped would eventually lead him to become a 'true preacher of God's
word… a real preacher; prophet, philosopher, poet – all in one.'

The Keswick Convention

Another 'turning point' in the development of Freeman's religious life was
his attendance at the Keswick Convention in July 1906. AJF, together with
his sister Elsie and their mother, joined the many thousands of Christians
who since 1875 attended the Keswick Convention and saw it as an opportunity for a deepening of their spiritual lives. For one week in July each
year the town of Keswick was transformed by a spiritual teaching that has
come to be regarded as one of the most significant in recent times.[14]

It is apparent from the diary that AJF attended Keswick to seek
assurance of his faith. He sought out two of the leaders of the Convention
to consult with them on his concern.

> Then I had such advice and teaching as I have not had for years.
> I could not understand exactly what conversion was. So far as I could
> see I had given my life to Christ… from what I could gather, the essen-
> tials to conversion or the reception of God's Holy Spirit are faith, a
> deep and overwhelming conviction of one's own sinfulness and a real
> desire to become absolutely empty for Christ to inhabit one's heart.

Despite the advice they gave him, Freeman still had doubts hanging over
him, and resolved to pray whenever doubt entered his heart. He came to
the conclusion that the way to illuminate his heart was not through the
intellect, which he had been striving to do, but rather, the intellect was to
be illuminated by the light of the heart. He also resolved that to become
aware of 'my sinfulness and my selfdom, I shall have made a grand step
onwards… to get in the habit of killing self and hating self – losing sight

entirely of self; to dislike praise, to be simply filled with the idea of glorifying Christ and Christ only'.

Later in the Keswick Convention Freeman experienced a conversion and became more deeply dedicated to what he perceived to be his mission in life; to serve Jesus Christ. The following extracts describe his conversion experience:

> After the meeting Moore asked those to stand who were Christian workers and had not yet received any experience of Christ. I felt this was a definite message to me and so stood up. Perhaps this may be called my conversion. At any rate I do believe that I have Christ in me, though as yet I feel nothing; I walk by faith and not by sight; I have received Christ, I have surrendered my life entirely to his use and entertained no willing sin; I am convinced of the utter worthlessness of my works and realise that by faith and not by works can I be saved and so believe that I have the gift of eternal life and have got into me the life that is life indeed – have ceased to live so that Christ may live in me. I resolve henceforth to subject my will in all things to Christ, always looking to Him for guidance and doing the work, whatever, wherever and whenever it may be that I think he would have me do. And I pray that he would grow and grow more in me and that self may grow less and less and that I may be allowed to do enormous work in glorifying His name.
>
> ———
>
> Yes it is marvellous, it is as if I had been living in the dusk all my life and now a flood of brilliant light has come into my soul and the world looks different… God has revealed to me himself and myself.
>
> ———
>
> I discovered that previously all I had done for Jesus had been done for selfish motives. Then I took my stand and resolved to begin a new life, realising that by faith and not by works are we saved… Christ began to live in my heart and since then has become more and more to me. I have seen my character transformed… I have seen my impure desires disappearing. I have found myself growing wondrously sympathetic and tactful and courteous and loving.

He left the Convention believing that all the world's social, religious and political problems would be solved by the presence of God's Spirit and by propagating the Gospel of Jesus Christ and that 'all worldly things must be transformed by the power of God's Spirit and not by human and independent efforts. We can do all things through Christ which strengthen us and without Him we are nothing and can do nothing'. He recognised that he remained a 'spiritual babe' but had found a treasure which would guide him away from the struggle of moral perfection to a belief that the right thing to do was let 'Christ grow in me'.

AJF returned to London, where he spent time with the extended family telling them about his conversion experience, believing that it impressed them, 'but not as much as I could have wished'. He later argued with his mother, Elsie, Ted and his wife Annie about faith and salvation. They believed 'in the comfortable doctrine that everyone is going to heaven', but for Arnold everything depended on faith in, and union with Christ.

At the end of August, he spent two weeks in Penarth with his father, Peter, Daisy and Dolly; walking, swimming, praying and eating. Besides cycling and football, walking was the activity most mentioned in his early diaries. For example, after his visit to Penarth he went on a long trek through the Wye Valley with his brother Peter, starting in Chepstow, travelling on to Bigsweir, Monmouth, Symonds Yat and then doing a loop through Welsh Bicknor and round to Lydbrook. They travelled south to Broadwell and back on to their original route at Bigsweir and on to Chepstow where they boarded the train back to Penarth. He had had a rewarding summer, which brought his return to university into sharp relief.

Just before his return to Oxford for his second year of study, the 20-year-old Arnold reviewed his position, in order to take 'a look back a little and look forward and also see precisely where I stand now.' In particular he wished to review his position on baptism, which clearly illustrates his depth of religious feeling and the direction he felt his life should take. He mentioned, for example, that with regard to his baptism he wanted 'to make a full and deep consecration of myself to my Saviour's work… a complete surrender to Christ… it is a means of power and grace. Christ did nothing miraculous until he had been baptised, only then did the Holy host descent upon him.' He viewed his own baptism as the most definite step in his whole 'eternal existence… all I have and all I am are laid upon the Cross for His glory.' His deepest desire was to give himself up completely to God's work, he felt that God was 'looking upon me and asking me to let Him work a revolution through me'.

This point in his 1906 diary also contains a retrospective account of events that ignited 'the divine spark that could be blown into a consuming flame by the breath of the Master'. The 'first distinct impetus' to this attitude, he identified as his reading of David Copperfield, the semi-auto-biographical novel by Charles Dickens. Other factors include the positive influence of his parents and teachers and the great love and pride he felt for his school. Also significant was his acceptance at St John's College, (news broken to him by his sister Elsie while he was having a bath), meeting Marsh Roberts who introduced him to Keswick, and his friend Horace who guided AJF to resolve 'that by faith and not works are we saved'. 'Here then', he writes, 'the old Arnold Freeman-like Hyde writes his last words. I am going to be buried with Christ in baptism and I shall be raised again with a new body, even to body of Jesus.'

Evangelism, Disillusion and Decision

Freeman's depth of religious feeling and the notion that he was singled out for a specific purpose and mission in life help explain his motivations during the following months at university. What had changed for him was his attitude towards Oxford University. Initially, he was hostile to its values; thought the institution hypocritical and the privileged students seduced into hedonism. Now by contrast, in the aftermath of his baptism, he resolved to change this attitude, for, 'to transform a university – just as to transform an individual – one must believe in it.' So Freeman, Marsh Roberts, his American friend and Rhodes scholar Mohler and Jessop together began their mission to spread the Christian word throughout St John's, initially by talking to other students about religion at least once a week and by recruiting 'ardent Christians' into Freeman's Society for Active Christians. One afternoon they also took thirty copies of Drummond's *Greatest Thing in the World* and distributed them to 'the chaps' at Ruskin College.

Driven by his devotion to changing the world by preaching, halfway through the 1906 autumn term AJF began to reflect on his course of study and whether it would be better to concentrate more on his religious aspirations to become a minister. He made an appointment to have tea with Sidney Ball and revealed to him his doubts about his motivation to complete his degree because 'cramming for the history school would undermine what reasoning faculty I had.' Ball suggested to him that he might want to concentrate on political science and political economy; write for one of the prizes or take the Diploma in Economics.' Freeman was sure he would only pass the degree, go on to Mansfield College and then work along his 'own lines'. 'I hate the idea of becoming an intellectual dustbin', the priority for him was to learn to think, write and speak.

His plans and worries about the future were exacerbated by the on-going problems with his throat. As an alternative to giving sermons Freeman went to see Reeves from the Salvation Army 'with whom I have arranged for lessons on the concertina. If I cannot speak at least I can play the concertina and give away tracts.' He felt a little aggrieved 'against God for not giving me back my voice, but I can see it is better so, but for my many failures here I should never have come to know Jesus as I do'. He doubted whether he would ever have a strong throat again and asked: 'what will constitute my occupation I do not know. It is in God's hand. I shall live like a rat in some attic and write'. Whatever path he would take, it would not be conventional, as Freeman refused to waste time 'on earning money in any ordinary profession unless Christ asks me to do so'.

AJF often went home to London at weekends to spend time with family and friends. A typical weekend at home in mid-February 1907 saw him at the theatre with his mother watching George Bernard Shaw's *The Doctor's Dilemma* which he said was 'an attack on the credulity of man in trusting doctors. All the characters are either heartless or brainless.' On Sunday morning he heard 'two grand sermons' from John Henry Jowett (1864-1923), a leading Congregationalist reputed to be the most appealing preacher in England. He then spent time with the extended family and travelled back to Oxford on Monday afternoon.

The two academic terms of 1907 were for AJF a time to consolidate
his decision to lead a 'Christ Like Life' and above all to put this into
practice. For example, he and his close friend Marsh Roberts went
regularly to the district of Jericho, which was then the poorer working-
class area of Oxford, to lead 'a little evangelistic meeting by a public house.'
Freeman tells us that on one particular evening 'it was bitterly cold; far
below freezing with a thin layer of snow on the ground. Marsh organized
everything and read from a text whilst I gave away tracts, including some
to the public house. We had a struggling audience of passers-by and of a
few loiterers at the doors'. He also went down to the Martyrs Memorial
holding out a collection box for the Salvation Army, who he thought were
'fine people… there is nothing artificial or sentimental about them; all
their proceedings are characterised by a healthy, hearty, homely spirit.'

Among the many conversations he had during this period, AJF pays
special attention in the diary to one with Joseph Estlin Carpenter (1844-
1927), a Unitarian minister and the principal of what was then Manchester
College in Oxford. Carpenter made an impression on him because they
both recognised that they were 'seeking after the same truth, the same God.
If only men and women would come to recognise that the one supreme
thing is Love.' His reading of Augustus Jessops's (1823-1914) *Coming of
the Friars* helped confirm his conviction that his life was destined to be a
life of serving Christ. After reading it he felt that God had spoken to him
again and that 'for years deep down in my heart my great longing has been
to serve Him.'

Freeman not only had conversations with ministers who were in
sympathy with his views, but others with whom he vehemently disagreed.
For example, he once argued with three members of the Church of
England, or 'High Churchmen' as he called them. Their discussion focused
on communion and the taking of the sacrament. Freeman recalls how they
believed it was actually the material flesh and blood they ate 'by some
wonderful, miraculous multiplication of our Lord's earthly body.'

What I kept grinding on to them about was their reverence for
material. They think of the matter and not the Spirit in the

Communion; of the visible church and not the spiritual society in
the Kingdom; of a bodily and not a spiritual resurrection.

Freeman still saw himself as dissenter, because he believed there was as
much spiritual work done by dissenters as there was by those in the
Anglican establishment. From his late teens he had always rebelled against
orthodoxy and this is the main reason why he, with the support of his
family, wanted to study at Mansfield College. Originally, the College's
purpose had been to educate students from a Congregational background
who rejected the hierarchical structures of the Anglican Church in favour
of the self-government of local churches, and it was just such a church
that Arnold envisioned for his future. But by mid-June 1907 there were
some discernible changes occurring in AJF's intellectual and emotional
life. After taking his entrance examination for Mansfield he went before
the board to ask for a stipend of £30 a year but they refused him, telling
him to apply later 'presumably because I already have £110 and they are
hard up. Have since thought seriously that it would be better for me not
to go to a Theological College at all. Is this the Hand of God confirming a
course I have often considered more useful?' As a result of this rejection,
Freeman began to reconsider his whole future, and his decision was aided
by going to a dinner at Mansfield. He was 'rather disgusted with it: four
courses, fancy dishes, Latin grace and all the men trying to be academically
witty. There is an awful lack of spiritual fervour that comes from much
waiting on God at Mansfield. Is Campbell right in saying that the only
theological College is worse than useless.'

Three months later when walking with a friend they decided to go
to Germany together to study theology:

> We are both sick with the Mansfield sausage-machine. I fear that
> their not taking me last term is, in the traditional phraseology,
> providential. My latest idea is to have a fourth year here and take the
> diploma in economics. Then have a partial year of knocking
> about… then go to Germany for two years, write my thesis for PhD
> and spend several months travelling about.

This plan never came to pass, and although Freeman did make two trips to Germany they were not for studying but for leisure: the first in September 1908 for a holiday and the second in 1911 to visit Ernst Haeckel and Rudolf Steiner.

During these months of change AJF went on holiday in Norfolk where he visited the Ruskin School Home in Heachem founded by Bellerby (Harry) Lowerison (1863-1935), who was an early member of the Fabian Society serving on the national Executive from 1891-1892. Freeman described his meeting and conversation with Lowerison in some detail.[15] Lowerison, he writes:

> Lives in a little cottage and gave us a cordial welcome. He looked like a Socialist, with his long hair and beard and his tie knotted anyhow… he talked in the easy abandoned way that comes from much experience of the world… soon after he volunteered the wish that religion could be cleared out of life altogether.

Because of his involvement with the Fabian Society, Lowerison told Freeman that he knew George Bernard Shaw very well and was very familiar with the works of Campbell. The Ruskin Home School was established in 1899 after Lowerison was dismissed from his post at Wenlock Road School in Hackney as a result of his letter writing to the socialist newspaper *The Clarion*. It was here that he outlined the principles on which he would found the School. He was helped in doing this mainly from donations and loans from the readers of *The Clarion*. He told Freeman that when he started the school, he experienced hostilities from the 'Christian' neighbours who 'smashed the bloody Socialist's windows and rooted up his fruit trees'. Lowerison told him in some detail the educational methods he employed at the school:

> His method is not to teach boys but to help them grow. He takes subjects in which all the boys and girls are interested… he has a curriculum but is not bound by it… he consults his pupils on all the work, encourages them to ask questions about everything… most of his lessons are conducted in the open air… they do plenty of

gardening… he teaches them to think and understand; teaches them to learn for themselves… he quoted Emerson also, who said that you can teach children more in playing with them than in working with them.

Freeman was keen to return to the school and work as a volunteer as Lowerison had explained to him that sometimes he didn't know where the money was coming from to pay his teachers the next day and many times he considered shutting the school, but money always came at the last moment.

This visit stimulated some thoughts for Freeman's future, and he began to consider his priorities for the months ahead. The main priority was to sit and pass his examinations, but the exams hung over his head 'like a sword and prevents me doing as I would'. Beyond things like learning to write and speak better in order 'to do active evangelising work without scruple', Freeman looked forward 'to a church or a school or a settlement or literary work or all of them'. He was also determined to work hard on his character to achieve a 'loving, energetic and influential' disposition, by prayer and positive thinking, as 'it is thought that makes character.' By October 1907, we see that he had come to recognise that a change had taken place:

> I am going to say here for my own reference that in absolute sincerity I have changed my beliefs very much on the last year – or at any rate have come to much clearer definitions of what I believe. I am not conscious of any corresponding decline in character… at least I have especially kept the one ideal of Christ-like character as all important continually before my eyes.

The nature of these changes and how they impacted his life are explored later in the next chapter, but by August 1908 Freeman described how his ideal had 'changed much in detail but not so greatly in soul'. He still desired to be a vigorous, active, original man pouring forth life into the world; 'whatever happens I will be an agitator.'

Friendship and a Full Life

Reading the diaries of Freeman's life during his years at Oxford creates the impression of a continuous round of social activities interspersed with short periods of study. In particular, he made many new friends and one significant friendship worth mentioning was his relationship with Jack Lawson and his wife Bella. Jack Lawson (1881-1965) was a miner and trade unionist who was studying on a scholarship at Ruskin College.[16] He later became a Labour member of parliament for the constituency of Chester-le-Street, entering the House of Commons after a by-election in 1919. He remained an MP until his resignation in 1949 when he was appointed Lord Lieutenant of Durham. In March 1950 he was appointed Baron Lawson of Beamish. In 1932 he published *A Man's Life*, an autobiography that includes his reminiscences as a miner and his Oxford days, with a fresh chapter added in 1942 covering the events until that date. In this book Freeman gets a very brief mention when Lawson recalls his time at Oxford and how difficult it was for him and his wife financially. He writes that:

> By the middle of the year (1908) I was literally on the rocks as far as clothes were concerned. But I had made good friends, and two of them, Arnold Freeman, who has done great work in the Sheffield Settlement, and good-hearted Marsh Roberts tried artfully to come to the rescue. But there was nothing doing.

One can only assume that Freeman and Roberts, both renowned for their eccentric clothing tastes, either lent him or gave him some clothes, but Lawson's financial situation remained unresolved. Lawson at this time had been offered a further six months' scholarship, so after returning to the mines in Boldon over the winter he raised enough money to begin his second year of study in February 1908. In both the 1907 and 1908 diaries Freeman makes frequent references to Lawson and his wife Bella indicating the development of a close and firm friendship. For example, Lawson visited him regularly in London and on Friday 6th September 1907 he met Lawson at Paddington station to spend the weekend with Freeman's family. He notes the following:

We had many inspiring talks. Don was also up for the weekend and our house was converted into an eighteenth-century Coffee House and socialism was discussed all day long. Lawson did much to convert them too. His obvious honesty and earnestness and good sense, combined with his first-hand knowledge, made a distinct impression.

On another occasion they spent time walking around London sightseeing, going to Hyde Park to Speakers Corner and on the Sunday going to church together to hear a sermon by Clifford. Lawson, Bella, Freeman and friends often met for tea and games in Oxford and one time attended the first meeting of the Society for the Development of Spiritual Magnetism.

It is also apparent that his final undergraduate year at Oxford was not easy for Freeman, but in a different way from Lawson. He noted in July 1908 that:

I am supposed to be doing revision, but I find it hard. I have restrained myself for so many years, that now the exam is over, I cannot settle down again to revise the old stale stuff. I feel the longing for new experiences and vital work burning in my soul.

Also during July, Freeman worked for a week for the North London Guardian to experience life as a journalist and attended the North London Police Court to observe the proceedings from 'a solicitor's desk.' It was here, he explains that he 'realised vividly that there is a dark side to life which we in our comfort and blindness rarely see.' The darker side was when some men were being sentenced for drunk and disorderly conduct and Freeman reflected that the 'bloated old magistrate' was more deserving of punishment than those poor fellows.

On September 4th Freeman went on a cycling tour to Germany with cousin Jake. They travelled from Dover to Calais (he was sick on the crossing), then on to Brussels, Liege, Aachen and Cologne to see the cathedral where they 'saw a casket containing the bones of the three wise men of the east, worth seven million marks.' From there they caught a train to Rüdesheim, took a steamer to Königswinter and another boat to

Bonn and back to Cologne for an overnight stay. The next day they cycled to Neuss, where, due to punctures, Jake gave up cycling and took a train to Rotterdam whilst Arnold travelled further into Holland to visit Eindhoven and Breda and then back to Harwich via Rotterdam.

In October 1908 just before he started his postgraduate diploma in Economics at Oxford, Freeman attended one of George Bernard Shaw's Fabian lectures at Essex Hall where he met fellow Fabian Angelo Rappoport (1871-1950) who told him that Sidney Webb thought him a promising member. Two weeks later, back at Oxford, in a discussion with Sidney Ball he writes that he was in agreement about him taking the Diploma and 'was glad that I was going to work at the School of Economics'. This is the first mention Freeman makes about working at the LSE and it is likely he is referring to a conversation he had with Webb on September 22nd, where Freeman asked him about his chances of a DSc at the LSE. Webb responded by advising him to enter his name in April 1909 and to 'be considering a small subject.' Webb, he thought, was 'a most courteous man; dresses like a second-hand clothes dealer; doesn't speak like a genius; looks like a well-bred carpenter.'

Freeman was passionate about economics and decided to make his two special subjects for his Diploma the Victorian Era and the Socialist School of Thought. His course of study would take him from the Industrial revolution to then 'thrash out each problem in economics as it arises.' He was determined to 'understand economics inside out and to be able to make economic matters plain to the man in the street,' something he did later when working for the WEA.

The autumn term was filled with attendance at meetings, seminars, lectures, sermons and in October his graduation ceremony for his BA, which he said was 'a disgrace to the whole of the civilised nation. Whilst thousands are starving they kept us waiting for nearly two hours while they performed silly antics and gabbled Latin… I feel ashamed of having undergone the humiliation of graduating.'

Just to give a taste of how crowded his days were at Oxford during this term I will give a brief summary of some of his activities. On October 19th he visited several homes of the Society for Prevention of

Cruelty to Children and one evening he went to the Cosmopolitan Club where he met Hal Dayal, who became a close friend. Another day he attended a lecture by Professor Fiedler on Germany where he thought social democracy was more progressive. After his graduation he went to a boxing match and later, at a Ruskin College debate, spoke on 'Does Determinism Destroy Responsibility?' On Sundays he took his Sunday School class, something he did throughout his Oxford years. He still attended meetings of the Fabian Society and joined meetings of the Social Science Club. He became secretary of the Clarion Fellowship, received feedback from Sidney Ball on his essays, and back in London for a weekend, joined the Suffragettes when they stormed Holloway Prison. In Oxford he spoke at an Independent Labour Party meeting and the next day visited a slaughterhouse with Marsh, watched in disgust while some animals were killed and afterwards wrote home to his mother and his sisters to inform them with characteristic zeal, that he would not kiss them ever again until they gave up meat. One Saturday he visited a Jewish Synagogue, remarking that he had 'never been so kindly treated in any Christian place of worship as I was there. I think I shall become a Jew.'

Just before Christmas he visited 'Captain Jessel at the London Municipal Society which was formed in 1894 to support the pro-Unionist Moderate candidates in London local elections. Jessel was Herbert Merton Jessel, 1st Baron Jessel (1866-1950) a prominent member of the Jewish community in London, Lord Mayor of Westminster (1902-1903) and member of Parliament until he lost his set in the Liberal Landslide in 1906. Freeman was there to interview him, for what purpose it is not clear, but Freeman was determined to rebut Jessel's anti-socialist views. Jessel, however, tried unsuccessfully to recruit him to the conservative cause which he thought was probably the reason for Freeman's visit. In his diary AJF notes that he did not 'like the look of the man. He looked a drinking, swearing, womanising sort of man.'

On Christmas Eve he saw a performance at Sadler's Wells which he thought was rather poor, so this perhaps explains why they went to Piccadilly afterwards 'to see the prostitutes', but unfortunately he writes, 'we saw none,' but on the way home he told Peter a great deal about prostitution; 'the ignorance that exists on the subject is simply appalling'.

It was at the beginning of 1909 that Winfried Lines, his first love, terminated their relationship, while Freeman vowed to close his heart with a snap to love and open it to ambition, humour, work, literature, music, art, imagination and propaganda. Back in Oxford he instigated the founding of the Fraternity of Reason another of his 'freethinking societies' and on asking both Denis Hird and Sidney Ball to take on the Presidency they refused as they would 'both get into trouble'. At the end of January, the Committee of the Oxford Branch of the Independent Labour Party (ILP) invited him to become their prospective parliamentary candidate for the City of Oxford, which he says gave him the possibility of turning his thoughts to something big, but thought their support for him showed that they thought the party was unlikely to win the election. In March 1909 he published his one-and-only pamphlet: *The Superman*, which was, according to Freeman, 'being sold on the streets.' Just before he left Oxford, he decided not to stand for the ILP, without giving a concrete reason, although at the final meeting where he gave his 'election address' he relates that nearly two hours were taken up with stupid questions and discussion. 'I felt so sickened with the whole proceedings and with the repulsiveness of democracy that I believe I got up and spoke with a feeling not to become the candidate for Oxford after all.' He left Oxford on Thursday March 12th, 1909 for the Easter break, and went home to London with the aim of corrupting 'the youth in this home… and to do my best to turn them (the twins) into rebels.'

He returned in May to finish off his Diploma in Economics and to sit his final examinations. At the end of June, he recorded the following:

> So ends the Oxford chapter of my career. I went to Oxford full of enthusiasm for reform; narrow minded, sincere, ignorant and orthodox. I leave Oxford still full of enthusiasm for reform, but I leave it unorthodox, large minded, knowing much and knowing most how much I have to know yet. In the main I am just as I was four years ago. I have the same passion for helping others, perhaps

I have it ever more strongly. I have even less care for marriage or money than I had. But many of my old ideals have been crushed for me and I have lost much of the old reckless ardour. Oxford has broken down my old faith and I have to build a strong new religion.

Chapter Three
George Bernard Shaw

A Shifting Perspective

Beginning of an argument with Mother and Elsie at lunch about my outlook on life generally. There has been some little friction for some time. My ideas have changed and the virtue of strength which I apotheosise is the very one that Mother most lacks at this time. They also think that I am selfishly taking my own pleasure just now… I am sorry to hurt their feelings or upset their views, but I must pursue my way relentlessly.

(July 11th, 1908).

At the end of 1907 significant changes occurred in Freeman's inner life and the above quote demonstrates that by the middle of 1908 this was starting to cause tensions within the family. The year began with intense religious feeling, his visit to Keswick taught him a great deal and gave him experiences 'that will be of use later on.' His plans to be a minister of religion were rapidly fading, because of his loss of faith in the 'old Christianity'. He now looked forward to forging a career as a writer, through which he thought he could be of 'more service to the cause than as a minister.' (He had just finished reading Elizabeth Barrett Browning's *Aurora Leigh*, who also aspired to become a great writer).

The beginnings of this momentous inner change can be seen as early as mid-September 1907 when Freeman completed his paper on *A Plea for the Madman*, which is unfortunately no longer extant. During this period, he wrote that he scarcely knew what his religion was; whether he was an atheist, Unitarian or Christian, and that 'it seems to me that a man might be any of these and still be called orthodox.' Belief in God, the Divinity of Christ, salvation, heaven and hell meant little to him as he no longer felt that he knew with any certainty what they were. 'From this basis,' he wrote, 'I shall be able to build up my theories of religion and philosophy,' being disposed, as he was, more 'to the atheist than to the ordinary Christian.'

Freeman felt in these months that he needed 'to develop himself, to let my own individuality assert and unfold itself, heedless of all codes, standards and criticisms'. He wished to shed his 'persona' as a devout Christian and to 'drive the change in my belief from orthodoxy to heterodoxy.' Despite the accusations made against him, mainly by family members, he defended himself by asserting that his change in character took him 'from worse to better,' by leaving the 'substance of true religion and only casting away the shadow, the outward belief.'

At this moment in his life we see a complete break from Freeman's former religious fervour, and a shift in the whole of his outlook on religion, politics, careers and life in general. There could be many reasons why this inner transformation occurred when it did, but whatever the cause, the twenty-one-year-old was growing more independent in building his own vision for his future and exploring aspects of life he previously had not. But there was also a dark side to this development, for AJF behaved as though he were invincible; he became arrogant, conceited and, perhaps, too wildly enthusiastic about his newly discovered 'religion'. He wrote in March 1908 that he was progressing with his 'Magnum Opus', 'which ought to be published', as it was 'a cool enquiry into the pros and cons of life with the idea of finding a credible religion.'

This newly discovered 'credible religion' he found in the works of George Bernard Shaw (GBS).[17] It was Shaw's political philosophy, his religious outlook and especially his plays that inspired AJF. One of the first in-person impressions that he had of Shaw was when he attended one of his lectures in March 1908, reflecting afterwards that GBS was a 'very clear and convincing speaker and treats difficult questions with great skill.' What particularly impressed AJF was Shaw's argument that one can judge a nation by its conscience and what needed to be done was 'to give the nation a hygienic conscience, then an artistic conscience and finally a social conscience.' In the diary Freeman then recorded one of his classic character descriptions, describing Shaw as 'a tall thin man' that 'looks like an ascetic; like an austere Puritan more divine than the weird personality that most people shudder at when his name is mentioned'. As we shall see, GBS had a great influence on Freeman's turbulent outlook during this period and became one of his mentors, guides and inspirations for much of his life.

The Influence of George Bernard Shaw

George Bernard Shaw first appears in Freeman's diaries at Christmas 1906 when Freeman and his sister Elsie went to a performance of Shaw's *Man and Superman*. Freeman briefly summarised the persona of Jack Tanner, one of the main characters in the play, writing that 'he is a far sighted cynic with revolutionary social ideas, like Shaw himself.' He was particularly enthused by the way Tanner 'laughs at the whole filigree fabric of conventional society', and his advocacy of liberty of conscience, individual judgment and his 'snap' of 'fingers at the world.' This was a person whom Freeman could emulate as he saw in Tanner 'a defence of his own theories of life put pictorially before me.' Seeing the play made him more determined to formulate his own independent ideas and 'not be bound by the maddening structures of all the Mrs Grundys in creation.'

After reading George Bernard Shaw's *Three Plays for Puritans*, Freeman described them as follows:

> Magnificent: as he says he is not so much original, as an embodiment of the advanced thought of the age. Admiration of his character and intellect grows upon me. And I, going in for the Church! What is this age coming to?

And later he declared:

> If I take anyone today for a hero it will be George Bernard Shaw. The life I intend to lead will bear a resemblance to his. But I am going to be Arnold Freeman and no one else.

And just after being rejected by one of his 'lovers' he wrote that he would:

> Plunge into activity… this will greatly encourage me on my career
> as a champion against all forms of accepted religion. I will become
> far more of a cynic with regard to love and ladies and all other gentle
> things in life. Bernard Shaw! You have been more than mother and
> father and God Himself to me! You have made a man of me by your
> philosophy!

The diaries for this period contain many references to GBS and his plays, in particular to *The Devil's Disciple*, originally written in 1897 and later in 1901 published as *Three Plays for Puritans* together with *Captain Brassbound's Conversion* and *Caesar and Cleopatra*. On seeing *The Devil's Disciple* in London Freeman found it simply grand. 'I have never seen a play so thrilling and yet so free from all farce and melodrama. I resolved to go again if I went on my hands and knees.' And he did see it again the following week and again on Boxing Day. On Sunday December 1st 1907 he saw Shaw's *Candida* and he 'liked it better than any other of his I have seen, perhaps better than any other play I have seen. Of its kind it was better than Shakespeare.'

GBS was a dedicated Fabian socialist who wrote many of the early publications of the Fabian Society. Several of his plays, including *Mrs Warren's Profession* and *Pygmalion*, are underpinned by socialist politics, addressing issues such as women's rights, poverty and capitalism. He had a reputation of being a rebel, an iconoclast, a destructive critic, a propagandist and a socialist agitator. Throughout his life he was a tireless crusader against social injustice and unrighteousness.

The 'Socialism' Freeman articulated in his diaries aligns very closely with that of Shaw and the Fabian Society. Broadly speaking this vision of socialism includes a passionate commitment to social justice and deep social reform, and a belief in the progressive improvement of society. In this version of socialism there was no place for class warfare, but rather the socialist society was to be brought about by means of intellectual debate, the publication of books and pamphlets, and the permeation of socialist ideas into the universities, the press, government institutions and

George Bernard Shaw

political parties. Other main socialist principles, less evident in Freeman's diaries that he most likely supported all the same, include ideas about how differential access to land and capital created mutually hostile social classes, hence the need to nationalise land ownership; that capitalism needed to distribute its benefits in the fairest way attainable; and the need for direct taxation and a free and liberal education for everybody and equal political rights for women.

Shaw, besides being a confirmed atheist and implacably opposed to traditional church-based religion, also rebelled against established social norms and held an alternative perspective on the conventional gender relationship. So, it is not surprising that Freeman adopted as his role model Richard Dudgeon, the main character from *The Devil's Disciple*. Dudgeon turned his back on Puritanism, despised the religious hypocrisy of those around him and was generally a rebellious character. The main reason, however, why Dudgeon rebelled was because of his disgust at his mother's rigid piety. As an act of defiance, he fled this pious lifestyle for a life of freedom.

Following Dudgeon, Freeman was determined to shed his image of being a devout Christian and declared his agnosticism to the whole world. At the end of 1907 he revealed that 'the year has been one of conversion from the admiration of the heart to an admiration of the intellect or rather the imagination and from personal to social religion, largely under the influence of Bernard Shaw, Campbell and the tendencies of the day. I have become utterly unorthodox; I do not know my creed.' Freeman's family, meanwhile, were greatly distressed at this transformation from a religious idealist, who was ostensibly preparing for the ministry, to a contemptuous radical who criticised current morality and religious hypocrisy, who championed unpopular causes and vigorously supported the suffragette movement.

One day AJF took the twin Freeman sisters to visit the Suffragettes without his mother's permission and on their return home they were sent straight to bed and he was told that if he didn't start behaving then he could move out. His friend Kathleen wrote him a letter expressing her disappointment that he was rejecting his family and friends:

> Dear Arnold, it grieves me much that you are shunning all your old friends, friends, who if you only let them, would do the best to strengthen your faith… you read the works of agnostics and admire a man like Bernard Shaw… it cannot be Arnold that you do not wish to regain your faith… Agnosticism will bring you no happiness whatever.

Freeman's response to this was to say that he would inform everyone that he was now an 'infidel' and was completely convinced that the country was ripe for a revolution, 'England was never so pregnant as she is now.' His mother also wrote to him pointing out that on his last visit home he seemed rather unsympathetic. Again, he responded by saying that he was coming out as an absolute Devil's Disciple and, like GBS was convinced that 'orthodox religion is dead'. His brother Ted also took issue with his agnosticism and criticised him for a letter he wrote to their mother and for his method of propagating his ideas by 'trying to attract, amuse and shock people instead of being practical, solemn and prosaic.'

During this period AJF read W. H. Davies's book *Autobiography of a Super-tramp*, with a preface written by Shaw in which he says 'another effect of this book on me is to make me realise what a slave of convention I have been all my life. When I think of the way I worked tamely for my living during all those years when Mr Davies, a free knight of the highway, lived like a pet bird on titbits, I feel that I have been duped out of my natural liberty.' This was surely a sentiment that appealed to Freeman whose 'supreme object' was to remain 'free to have my own views and to be a madman as I please and free to give most of my time to spreading my ideals'. The book also made Freeman more certain of his religion of 'Philosophic Fanaticism… my wish is still to be a vigorous, active, original man pouring faith into the world… whatever happens I will be an agitator… but my views are too jagged to fit into any-shaped theological hole'. At this point Freeman was near convinced that he would not become a minister of religion. He did, however, speculate on his future and consider earning money by tutoring or lecturing at a polytechnic, but money was not his priority as he longed, like GBS, to be 'a fully-fledged agitator… making speeches, writing articles and giving away tracts'.

Tramps, Supermen and Eugenics

In December 1908, most likely inspired by the *Autobiography of a Super-tramp*, Freeman and his friend Marsh Roberts spent a weekend tramping to Paris and back, and afterwards visited Shaw at his home in Adelphi Terrace. They were shown into the sitting room by the maid and Shaw entered ten minutes later. Freeman describes their meeting as follows:

The room was furnished well and even luxuriously… there was the famous bust by Rodin over Shaw's writing table, another rough sketch by Rodin over my chair… there was a portrait of Nietzsche by the door and another, I think of Aylmer Maud… he shook our hands not caring a straw for our dirt… he was dressed in a well made light green suit, wore brown shoes and socks, a cream silk and almost invisible collar and a green silk tie… his eyes are always on the twinkle… he has an almost enchanting way of speaking and listening… I can quite imagine ladies falling in love with his face.

When Shaw asked them what they were doing they told him they were tramping and he advised them to introduce it at Oxford, as they weren't taking jobs away from those who really needed them. They discussed money, Shaw's earnings and the state of the country. Freeman suggested that a revolution was round the corner as ideas were changing so quickly but Shaw doubted it as 'it often appeared like that'. At the close of the conversation Freeman noted that they probably spent three quarters of an hour with: 'The greatest man living… to think that we have modified the brain that will produce some of the greatest plays ever written… if I could give my life to save his I would. But I would not sacrifice it to anyone else.' This last line conveys perhaps the most powerful implicit rejection of his family and their values.

In January 1909, shortly after his visit to Shaw, Freeman founded a 'Superman Society' at Oxford and began to study *The Revolutionist's Handbook*, an appendix to the play *Man and Superman*. In a letter to Tolstoy in 1909, Shaw made explicit his concept of 'Superman' and its attendant doctrine the Life Force. These themes run through most of his later plays and take final shape as the doctrine of Creative Evolution in his *Back to Methuselah*, published in 1921:

> To me God does not yet exist; but there is a creative force struggling to evolve an executive organ of godlike knowledge and power; that is, to achieve omnipotence and omniscience; and every man and woman born is a fresh attempt to achieve this object. We are here to help God, to do his work, to remedy his whole errors, to strive towards Godhead ourselves. In its odyssey to achieve fruition, the life force would create ever-higher forms of humanity-- supermen, super-supermen, supermen to the third power: When one instrument is worn out, I will make another, and another, and another, always more and more intelligent and effective.

Historical examples of such 'supermen' include Julius Caesar, Napoleon Bonaparte and Oliver Cromwell, who despite their greatness, Shaw defined as 'casual supermen' because they had their flaws and were unable to fulfil their full potential. What Shaw envisaged for the future was a new race of more mentally healthy and morally independent human 'Supermen' who would have the courage to continually strive for excellence. Everyone, according to Shaw is a potential superman who can hasten their evolutionary process by 'willing' their own upward development. Thus, the superman from Shaw's play possesses the qualities of a superior intellect, cunning and intuition, the ability to defy the obsolete moral codes of the Victorian era and other self-defined virtues.

For Shaw, superhuman beings would develop mainly through 'good and selective breeding' or eugenics, which would lead to a significant improvement of the human race and eventually, after the defeat of capitalism by socialism, a utopian society. In a paper read before a Sociological Society meeting in the London School of Economics on May 16th 1904, he stated that: 'There is now no reasonable excuse for refusing to face the fact that nothing but a eugenic religion can save our civilization from the fate that has overtaken all previous civilisations'.

Shaw's ideas on eugenics shaped Freeman's own on the subject and, as we shall see, these ideas influenced his interpretation of the psychology of adolescence in his book, *Boy Life and Labour* and later in his investigation at Sheffield into the Equipment of the Workers. AJF's introduction to eugenics took place on the 11th December 1908 when he attended a lecture on the subject by Caleb Saleeby (1878-1940), a leading eugenicist in this period who was influential in launching the Eugenics Education Society. Saleeby was also a member of the Fabian Society, championed the emancipation of women and believed in the compatibility of eugenics and social and political progress, later known as 'reform eugenics'. Although Freeman was disappointed in Saleeby's delivery of the lecture he was 'intensely glad that Eugenics is attracting so much attention... we shall never make Supermen except by breeding.' His attraction to eugenics explains the statement he made after visiting the Temple of Beauty during his tramp to Paris when he said that the great benefit of prostitution is 'that it aids in the sterilisation of many stupid couples, which is an exceedingly good thing'.

Inklings of a Socialist Utopia

The influence of Shaw during this time is clearly seen in Freeman's study of *The Revolutionist's Handbook*, but especially from the section on the Oneida Community founded in America in 1848 'to carry out a resolution arrived at by a handful of Perfectionist Communists that we will devote ourselves exclusively to the establishment of the Kingdom of God.' For most of his life Shaw was a utopian visionary who looked to the establishment of the Kingdom of God, a vision which can be found later in Freeman's own idea of 'utopia' when he took over the wardenship of the Sheffield Educational Settlement in 1918 which was 'to establish in the City of Sheffield the Kingdom of God'. Freeman's utopian ideals inspired him to investigate community living so he visited the Whiteway Colony, a small community located not far from Stroud, which was originally founded on utopian socialist ideals by the non-conformist Quaker journalist, Samuel Veale Bracher, and others who rejected the idea of private property. The community, founded in 1898, sought to organize its affairs as close as possible to Tolstoy's beliefs. They attempted, for example, to live an ascetic and simple life, preferring to be vegetarian, non-smoking, teetotal and chaste. The residents there were also Christian pacifists and advocated nonresistance in all circumstances. Later he visited Letchworth Garden City which was at the time the world's first Garden City. It was created as a solution to the squalor and poverty of urban life in Britain in the late 19th century, based on the ideas of Ebenezer Howard as published in his book of 1898, *Tomorrow: A Peaceful Path to Reform*. As he entered the community Freeman observed:

> The roads were lined with lovely half wild flowers. There was untold variety in the houses and the people were dressed each after their own fashion and their faces shone with health. It gave me an inkling of the Socialist utopia that we are toiling for.

Freeman and his friend Arthur stayed overnight and the next day were introduced to the Open Air School, founded and built in 1905 by Annie Jane Lawrence (1863-1953), a Quaker. The school was originally intended to be a school of philosophy but also offered subjects such as economics, psychology and political science for students who had already left school. They were also taught skills from the Arts and Craft movement. Freeman remarked that it was 'a striking experiment in modern methods of education'.

On leaving Oxford in 1909 Freeman became more explicit in his diary entries about his utopian vision for a socialist society. He wrote that all over the world 'the greatest thinkers and prophets are saying the same glad message. Utopias are written in sober sincerity as realisable for our children if not for us. We are talking calmly of a federation of the world… my dream is of a Great World Republic. I dream ever more vividly of a Socialised England.' His task, he thought, was to supply the 'spiritual dynamite', he longed to be 'endowed with miraculous spiritual powers' and was willing 'to dare everything for the sake of my ideals.' So, at this point in his life Freeman wished to combine theosophical ideas with GBS's political and social activism to vanquish capitalism from the world and replace it with his version of a socialist utopia.

George Bernard Shaw on Rudolf Steiner

Freeman's involvement with George Bernard Shaw was not confined to his youth, and the writer's influence lived on in him for many years, culminating perhaps in the 1945 foundation of a Shaw Society at the Settlement in Sheffield. Prior to this on 26th October 1944, AJF sent Shaw a copy of his booklet on Steiner's *Philosophy of Freedom*, which led to a short chain of correspondence between the two. A few days after receiving the booklet Shaw replied that 'this little book is an excellent primer for novices, though you should delete the monstrous statement that thought cannot err. As if thought could escape the fallibilities of thinkers.' He went on to say that 'Steiner has said nothing that I have not said better' and advised Freeman and his students to read the preface to *Methuselah* if they wished to remain up to date.

AJF, never shy of an argument, responded with the insistence that pure thought does exist as it comes 'from the world depths. It cannot be

anything else than trustworthy.' He then addressed GBS's theory of the
Life Force on which Freeman, through his study of Steiner, had come to
take a different perspective. He argued that if the Life Force was to exist
then Shaw had to admit that it was a spiritual being working alongside
other beings fulfilling their manifold functions, each in their own way.
These considerations, Freeman claimed, do not 'shatter Shavianism but I
do think that they suggest that it needs a few repairs.' Unsurprisingly, GBS
was not convinced by this, arguing that 'Steiner tries to disembody the
facts and make Spiritual beings into *Dei Ex Machina*, words, words, words.
No use. I prefer his moonshine about the proper time to sow garden seeds.'

Undefeated, Freeman later presented Shaw with a copy of Steiner's
The Philosophy of Freedom with the following poetic inscription that does
much to clarify his perception of Shaw in this later stage of his life:

> *O Shaw,*
> *George Bernard Shaw,*
> *Foremost of living writers,*
> *Noblest of living men,*
> *Prepare to meet thy God!*
>
> *Great art thou Shaw, but not yet perfect,*
> *Othello was great but credulous,*
> *Lear was great but vain,*
> *Hamlet was great but undecided,*
> *Thou O Shaw art great but weak in epistemology,*
>
> *In thy recent exchange with our warden,*
> *O Shaw,*
> *Thou did get the worst of it.*
> *Freeman worsted thee,*
> *Clearly, he knew of what he was talking,*
> *While, as for thee,*
> *Thou knewest not.*
>
> *We envisage thee,*
> *O Shaw,*

Nearing the gates of Eternity.
Fearful will it be for thee,
If the Apostle challenges thee as thou approachest,
Asking:-
What knowest thou of epistemology,
The science of sciences,
Thou who didst claim on Earth to be the all-wise??
Fearful will it be for thee
If thou canst only fumble and mumble;
Fearful will it be
If the gates are closed upon thee,

Not in derision
O Shaw,
But in pity,
We send thee this gift,
We thine admiring admirers,
We who love thee.
We send it that thou may acquire the foundations of knowledge,
That thou mayest establish Shavianism upon the solid rock of Steiner,

St. Peter smiling upon thee,
Followed by all of us from The Sheffield Educational Settlement.

Shaw was obviously not impressed by this gift and its presumptive, if not even insulting dedication, but he became decidedly animated by a loaf of bread sent to him by Freeman, created using the biodynamic principles set out by Steiner. In a letter to D. V. Barber, Shaw remarked that whilst Steiner's 'intellectual machinery' was of no use to him, he found it impossible to obtain 'good stone ground bread. Shop sweepings labelled *Hovis* do not satisfy me,' and the bread which Arnold sent, 'though a little hard baked had some nourishment in it.' GBS asked Barber if she could supply him with one or two loaves a week, but despite all efforts and considerable correspondence with Maurice Wood at Huby Farm near Leeds, who produced the bread, Shaw (probably due to post-War supply issues) was unable to obtain any. So, in a move typical of Shaw's cynicism, it was bread not words that came closest to persuading him of the virtues of Steiner's philosophy, but ultimately, he remained unmoved by Freeman's not inconsiderable powers of persuasion. Therein lies an example of the paradox of the relationship between these men; they may have been closer friends had Shaw been more sympathetic to Freeman's point of view, and yet, it was precisely Shaw's fierce independence of thought and action that so powerfully commanded Freeman's admiration, right from his first encounters of the great author's work, during his youth.

Chapter Four

Matters of the Heart

Falling in Love

The romantic attachments that figure most prominently in Arnold Freeman's diaries are those with Winifred Lines, Juliet Stuart Points and Nora White. While AJF did eventually marry Nora in 1914, up until that time his attitude towards marriage had been fickle and even hostile at times. From about his twenty-first year, he was fundamentally averse to the idea of entering into a fully committed relationship. He was certainly open to a dedicated and loving 'affair' but commitment was problematic to him as it threatened to restrict his beloved freedom. There are frequent references to this non-committal attitude in his writing on relationships, for instance: 'One can never be sure about love. It gets you when you are not looking. I am not sure that it can be escaped. But I want to avoid it if it is by any means possible.' He was convinced that marriage was usually a failure that 'cuts you off from all society… nothing could be more weak willed than falling in love and getting married.' He described how he 'trembles at the idea of a woman who would restrain me.' Just before sitting his final examinations at Oxford he said if he didn't fall in love he would 'be all right… but at least I will not sacrifice my life for a wife. If it is a question of Life or Wife, I know which must go.'

Paradoxically, as we shall see in this chapter, Freeman was not afraid to propose marriage, despite never quite making up his mind as to whether he was in favour of it. His ambiguous attitude towards marriage can be seen for example, in 1910, when he resolved to lead a purer life; completely shun conventional relationships and avoid marriage at all costs.

Nevertheless, he formed a close relationship with an older woman called Margaret, saying of her that, 'she gives me the womanly sympathy and love that every man needs in his life… God has brought us together… I admire her more than any other woman I have ever known.' While he dreamt of sharing a home with her, he didn't seek marriage, preferring instead something like a small 'family' community together with other friends.

However, AJF's views were not his alone. His stance on marriage corresponded closely to that held by his heroes, such as George Bernard Shaw, as outlined in the preface to Shaw's play *Getting Married*.[18] Shaw argued that marriage is the subject on which the most dangerous nonsense is talked about: 'if the mischief stopped at talking and thinking it would be bad enough; but it goes further, into disastrous anarchical action'. He believed in love but not in marriage; he rooted for love and union of two souls in love, but he ridiculed the need to warrant acceptance from others by signing some legal contracts and saying 'I do' in church. As Shaw put it, 'the institution of marriage is unreasonable and inhuman to the point of utter abomination… there is no magic in marriage. If there were, married couples would never desire to separate. But they do.'

Unsurprisingly, Freeman's approach to courtship also seems to have been unconventional for his time. The diary entries about his romantic attachments appear to flout the 'strict rules' of courtship one encounters in popular novels, or modern film or television costume dramas. In comparison to the accepted view that, for example, a woman could not introduce herself or speak to a man without the correct introduction, or that a chaperone had to be present when a woman met a man, or a courting couple was not allowed to touch until after engagement, Freeman's relationships appear to have been much more relaxed and the women he associated with did not fit the stereotypical picture of the virginal ideal.

AJF's ideas of what constituted 'love' and 'love making' was also ambiguous. His diaries impart a sense of the wild fluctuations in his feeling life with regard to his romantic partners, from a state of torment to a disorienting and deep infatuation. It seems he thought that if a woman took a genuine interest in him and there was mutual attraction then this constituted a kind of 'love'. Freeman saw forms of love and 'love making' in gestures as vague as the placing of a hand on his arm, a certain kind of smile, an intimate conversation or the reception of a gift. For the young and inexperienced AJF, these could all be indications that 'she loved me'.

Winifred Lines

Freeman's first 'true love' was Winifred Lines (1890-1983) who was the daughter of Joseph Lines, the co-founder of G and J Lines Toy manufacturers, and sister to the three Lines brothers, William, Arthur and Walter who later founded their own toy manufacturing company (Tri-ang Toys) after returning from the First World War, becoming one of the largest toy manufacturers in the world. Winifred wasn't involved in the business, but received a good education and her father made sure she was looked after on his death.

Freeman's friendship and eventual 'love' for Winifred developed over a period of about three years when they met between term times and on the occasional weekend when he was home from Oxford and she from Boarding School. He was a regular visitor to the *Chantry*, the Lines's home at 141, Lordship Road just a ten-minute walk from his own home in Woodberry Down, and sometimes he would accompany her on trips to Barnet where she attended painting classes. The first 'real starting point' of his 'more serious and mature affection' for her began while on a walk around the Reservoir with her, her sister Edie and Mrs Lines, when she placed a 'gentle and momentary pressure of her hand' upon his arm. A sign for him that she deliberately wanted to show affection and the only indication he had for months that she cared for him.

However, his relationship with her was frowned upon by his own mother and older sister Elsie who 'lectured' him because he showed her 'too much affection' which they warned would make so deep an impression on her 'that she will fancy herself in love'. But initially their fears were unfounded because he was 'not in love with Winnie, but I am very fond of her and I admire her much more than any other girl I know.' Freeman did entertain the idea of how it would be to marry her but his views on marriage were protean and he used his diaries to tentatively explore how he felt about long-term relationships, especially the 'finality' of marriage. He abhorred the idea that he might marry a woman who would restrain him from living out his ideals, but conversely, would still consider a wife who was in sympathy with his work. He knew Winifred sympathised with most of his social and political ideas, but her father thought he was 'a little dotty'. Despite this, he remained on good terms with the whole Lines family.

These conflicting desires, on the one hand being increasingly drawn to Winifred and the prospect of a long-term and loving partnership, and on the other hand not wanting to be tied down by the confines of marriage, caused Freeman's relationship with Winifred to develop into 'a curious, interesting and difficult problem'. It is in his reflections on marriage and relationships that we discover a certain lack of self-knowledge on his part. He claimed for example that he had a 'too highly developed moral passion' to 'fall in love too easily', which is strongly contradicted by the evidence of his diaries.

An example of this and what he termed 'love making' can be found in his account of a visit to the Lines home on the evening of Tuesday December 15th, 1908, when he and Winifred 'luxuriated' for an hour or more in one of their playful conversations. He tells us that he had been secretly in love with her for more than two years, since she was sixteen. The talk turned to the subject of whether it would give him a 'thrill' to put on her boots for her and he speculated whether such an act may be called 'love making':

> As I sat there I could not help feeling that it was remarkably near to it. I think Winifred, like all ladies, tries to provoke me into saying what I feel about her. I never say outright that I love her, though we often talk in a joking, half distant way about love making, though now and then an involuntary reference half betrays our feelings towards one another.

On a different occasion he gives us a glimpse of his idea of 'love making' when he is alone with her at the Chantry. Her sister Edie had just gone upstairs so he stood near the mantelpiece so he could see her face better and 'talked in a way that bordered perilously near to love making'.

George Lines with his family.
Winifred Lines is on the far right.

By the New Year of 1909, just before his return to Oxford, Freeman resolved to write a letter to Winifred asking for her hand in marriage. So on Tuesday January 19th he began writing to tell the whole history of his love for her 'from the moment I first saw her in the scullery at the Chantry three years ago.' He told her of his ideal for a home, of having beautiful children 'that I hoped to bring up to such perfection'. He invited her to join him in a 'happy, useful life' and suggested that she spend the summer with him in Oxford.

He waited impatiently for an answer, thinking constantly of Winifred and even 'skipping' to her name. At last the postman arrived: 'I trembled with excitement to see Winifred's darling scrawl on the envelope and hurried upstairs to read it.'

Dear Arnold, Your letter absolutely astounded me. In fact the whole thing seems more like a dream than anything else. First, when I saw all the writing, I thought, 'What on earth has Arnold got such a lot to write about.' Then I thought somebody was playing me a practical joke and trying to be funny, but when I got to the end I came to the conclusion it must be from you… I'm not the slightest bit like what you make me out to be, and your idea of me is quite wrong.

She went on to say that if she had known he would fall in love with her she would have immediately 'nipped it in the bud and snubbed you like mad.' She added that 'you make me feel like one of those women who attract men and then make fools of them,' she was willing to be friends 'but nothing else.' Freeman went through the full cycle of grief, eventually admitting that he had probably hypnotised himself 'into adoring her and I can hypnotise myself out again'. He managed to remain philosophical about the whole affair and was thankful for his unorthodox views, saying that Christianity would have left him 'weak and praying at a time like this, worrying other people and bothering God. 'Nietzscheanism' has taught me to stand on my own feet and defy God and the world'. But he was still deeply hurt and to assuage the pain he resolved to:

Plunge into activity… this will greatly encourage me on my career as a champion against all forms of accepted religion. I will become far more of a cynic with regard to love and ladies and all other gentle things in life. Bernard Shaw! You have been more than mother and father and God Himself to me! You have made a man of me by your philosophy!

He also attempted to lessen his pain by denigrating the idea of marriage with Winifred, deciding it would mean living an 'unhealthy, immoral, cramped cat and dog' life. Drawing inspiration from Shaw's views on marriage he wrote how much luckier he was 'than John Tanner in *Man and Superman* who is persuaded to marry Ann' and he quoted from the final lines of *Captain Brassbound's Conversion*, '*What an escape*', adding 'I shall not have to join the crowd of greasy husbands with fishy eyes'.

Juliet Stuart Poyntz

Freeman's attachment to Juliet was quite different to his relationship with Winifred. In his diaries AJF painted Winifred as vulnerable, innocent, artistic (she painted and played piano), even-tempered, honest and someone open to his ideas. Juliet, on the other hand, while not Winifred's complete opposite, came from a very different social, cultural and educational background. Denise Lynn offers the following background story:[19]

> Juliet Stuart Poyntz was born Juliet Stewart Points in Omaha, Nebraska on 20th November 1886 to John J. Points and Alice Points. As an adult, Poyntz would use various iterations and spellings of her given name. Her attorney claimed she changed it as a college student to declare her independence. Poyntz grew up in a middle-class, educated family with strong roots in progressive politics, public service, and education; all values that were impressed upon her and that would influence her throughout her adult life. In 1897, Alice took her two daughters and left her husband, heading back east and settling in Jersey City, New Jersey. What happened in the Points' marriage is not clear, but they never legally divorced. It is also not clear whether the Points' daughters had any contact with their father after the move. Juliet Stuart Poyntz' lawyer, Elias Lieberman, later claimed that Poyntz came from a broken home and was raised primarily by her mother with no father figure at all. She was ten-years-old when her parents separated and she, her sister, and mother moved halfway across the country to New Jersey.

Lynn tells us that 'as a student, in primary and secondary school and college, Juliet was very active and engaged, often participating and sometimes taking the lead in school events (and) after graduating the eighth grade, she went to Dickinson High School where she proved to be exceptionally smart and motivated.' She was also involved in the promotion of women's education and gained a raft of honours at High School including 'the Dickinson medal, awarded annually to the student with the highest average in all four years of school.'

In the autumn of 1903, she entered Barnard College as a freshman in Manhattan, New York. One important factor in her education related by Denise Lynn was that Juliet 'attended college during the Progressive era when young women like herself, would be attracted to political reforms. Progressivism was a "catch-all" movement that encompassed a variety of reforms, but one thing Progressives had in common was the desire to "reshape society." Progressives focused on a variety of issues like immigration, and the effects of industrialization and urbanization.' Her involvement in this 'movement' obviously reinforced her desire for social change, and her later radical views on reforming society; something we can see in her conversations with Freeman.

In 1910 Juliet was awarded a prestigious scholarship sponsored by the General Federation of Women's Clubs. The scholarship applications were 'under the exact forms' by which the Rhodes scholarship was considered and the officers of the Rhodes trust examined the applicants. The final credentials of the candidates were decided by the General Federation, but their ultimate goal was to identify a woman with the 'highest promise of distinction'. The scholarship provided funds for a full year of study at an institution of the young woman's choice in England. Poyntz chose to study at the London School of Economics and Oxford where she conducted research on the industrial revolution and 'its bearing upon the labour of women.' Poyntz wrote later that it was a 'most illuminating experience' and she met some 'very interesting people'.

(Freeman at this time, besides working at the LSE, was involved in the Theosophical Society and was seriously considering traveling to Chicago to study under the supervision of the guru John E. Richardson otherwise known as TK who was introduced to him by Sean Williams. We shall hear more about this in the next two chapters).[20]

It was in this context that on Monday May 15th 1911, Freeman first met Juliet. He was attending a meeting at the London School of Economics to discuss a volume of essays that were eventually published as *Seasonal Trades*. He was joint editor in this enterprise with Sidney Webb and was responsible for meeting with the other authors and providing Webb with notes, ideas and material. Juliet eventually wrote the introduction to this volume. He relates the following story:

> Called at the LSE en route for Oxford to see Miss Juliet Stuart Points... we discussed her paper for the forthcoming volume... then began to talk of other things, America, Socialism, Oxford etc. I asked her what Chicago was like and said I thought of going out there.

Freeman offered to take some heavy books for her to Oxford where she was staying and 'after a friendly altercation... she suddenly asked me if my brother and I would come to tea tomorrow.' Freeman gladly accepted. They travelled to Oxford and subsequently had tea and he suggested she go to hear theosophist Annie Besant, discovering in the course of their conversation that Juliet was an agnostic, but believed in thought transference. That evening he and his brother Peter attended Besant's lecture on *The World Religion and the World Teacher* when suddenly Juliet appeared and sat with them. Afterwards she gave her opinion and said she thought the lecture was too full of generalities, but told them her father was a theosophist.

Juliet Stuart Poyntz

So began Freeman's second significant 'romantic attachment' and he declared: 'How odd it is that the person in my Seminar in whom I am "keen", I meet in this intimate way by a series of accidents. I confess I am delighted. I am not in love with her, but I love her and would like some long talks with her... I mean to turn this acquaintanceship into a life-long friendship.' He speculated that perhaps he could gain her interest in TK and maybe in the distant future marry her! In the following weeks he met with her frequently and one day, in London, after dining with her at a

Eustace Miles (1848-1948) restaurant he discovered that they shared
similar political convictions:[21]

> She thinks that one should throw oneself absolutely into the social
> movement... and she thinks it a waste of time to worry about God
> and the Future Life... she feels I am wasting my ability on a
> useless cause... she thinks we ought to concentrate on building
> the Socialist State.

Afterwards they spent six hours talking together and ended the day in
Hyde Park where the conversation turned to prostitution. Juliet revealed
she had visited the Leicester Lounge, a well-known place where prostitutes
'wait for their victims', and thought of writing a book on the whole issue.

Their friendship developed over the course of many meetings and
Freeman was completely captivated by the qualities and charms of Juliet.
However, his emotional response to the relationship was excessive given
their circumstances. For example, from the end of July, and throughout his
August holiday in Cornwall, approximately twenty-five pages of the diary
are dedicated to his reflections on his relationship and his deeper feelings
towards Juliet:

> Her smile is most captivating. I remember noticing its sweetness
> early in our acquaintanceship when I met her in the Common
> Room at the School... to put it bluntly I have a strange feeling –
> that sort of feeling that seems to occupy massively the whole of
> one's life – that Joan of Arc and I are falling in love with each
> other... there are little things that one can't describe in detail, that
> make me think she is fond of me... an inflexion of the voice... little
> fleeting touches... and I have already considered the greatest detail
> – the important problem of our suitability to one another... I must
> confess candidly that she is the closest approximation I have ever
> met to my ideal.

They affectionately addressed one another in their letters as Joan of Arc
and St. Francis. In mid August while on holiday in Cornwall he re-read his
diary and remarked 'she has cropped up persistently all through my

diaries… mingled with vows of celibacy, come innumerable assertions of vows of matrimony… there are times when I long for Joan of Arc and want her before the next life.' She wrote frequently to him about her paper in *Seasonal Trades* but always with an affectionate tone. For example one letter reads: 'I enjoyed your letter immensely – found it a refreshing diversion from seasonal trades and I will answer it when I can give it the time it deserves.' The promised letter came while he was still in Cornwall. Freeman reproduced it in its entirety, as it was not quite what he expected. It begins with a note of how envious she is of him of being in Cornwall 'in the midst of sea breezes. If you would see this thick, muggy, misty hot air you would understand why this letter won't sound inspired.' She continues:

> No I don't think I have recovered from youth. I have simply arrived at the age of youth tempered with discretion, which you may reach at the age of 35 (men are always ten years younger than women) unless you go to America where men, like Peter Pan, never grow up. Did I say I had relinquished the idea of accomplishing great things, I only meant *great things* according to your definition or according to your feeling-dramatic, soul stirring, Victor Hugo-esque great things. But I hope to be of even greater use in the world than if I did great things. You see the theory of *great things* goes along with the theory of *great men* in history and both, I think, have been explored. But a theory is just as good for religious purposes… because they don't deal with facts or reason. Is it not so? No, my good St. Francis, never, never, never! Never could I be religious. That doesn't mean I couldn't be spiritual or idealistic or anything else, but I have an inherent and deep-seated aversion and distrust of the religious method. More than that, I have a real personal dislike of it – which has increased since I have been in England… religion to my mind is simply laziness… my father (the type and epitome of laziness) landed in theosophy through that weakness… and might have been a socialist if he had kept on thinking.

She went on to say that there were exceptions to her general analysis and Freeman was one. He was not religious because he was lazy but was young and impatient, 'like a little boy building a house of bricks who finds the operation too long for his impatience and too rational for his impulsiveness and demolishes the whole thing with a vicious blow'.

She recognised his imagination and intuition but thought he had the 'American instinct of wanting to "get there too quick."' She then addressed something very close to Freeman's heart:

> As to TK I anticipate disillusionment… I expect you will find him either a fool or a knave, probably the former… he'll probably be a benevolent gentleman… who talks too much and says little, has his mouth full of scientific phrases which he does not understand.

She admitted to being 'frank' but asserted that a young man of Freeman's qualities, full of spirit and potentialities, 'could go off on a wild goose chase… but I am not afraid you will come round. You have too much sense, too much discrimination… forgive me for stating these plain truths so barely and even violently. You'll wake up soon!'

At first Freeman found the letter 'was a shock to the love feeling I held for Miss J.S.P.' and it lowered his opinion of her, deciding that her intellect was not as discriminating as he had first thought and describing her atheism as a 'bias' rather than a 'reasoned attitude.' On the second reading, however, Freeman claimed to have roared with laughter over her 'frank honesty with which we differ from one another'. He was, of course, upset by her remarks about TK, and suggested that if she had really read his books she would have recognised 'his powers'. Thus, he was thrown into an interrogation of his perceptions of her and questioned whether she was really as virtuous as he thought. 'Married life', he said, 'would be impossible with a person who was constitutionally incapable of comprehending the work to which I am devoting my life.'

With just one letter, his conception of Juliet was transformed from a possible marriage partner into an enigma whose 'pluck, purity and perseverance' he nevertheless admired. Hoping that her attitude may be transitory, Freeman decided to invite her to lunch, in order to 'correct these impressions.' A few days later he received an invitation from her to meet him at Eustace Miles on Thursday 31st of August, in which she tells him that he 'is a refreshing person… how did you ever contrive to be born in England?'

Apparently the lunch at Eustace Miles didn't happen and Juliet failed to turn up at another lunch at Shearer's because of a trip to Dieppe. Meanwhile, Freeman was seriously thinking of asking Juliet to marry him and although he didn't think he loved her he was convinced that his admiration for her would eventually turn into love, though he continued to equivocate about his feelings for her:

> She is always cheerful and attentive and collected and cool. She never speaks stupidly but she is never grandiloquent. She is always sympathetic but always independent. She is always serious but never lacks the sense of humour. I am beginning to make her out as a Goddess. Something that I can fall in love with… The strange thing is that I am doubtful if I am really in love… if she were to show me unmistakably that she did not care for me in the romantic fashion, I should say 'Thank God' that I escaped to America still a free man… And yet if she gives me the greatest hint that she loves me, I shall tell her in the instant that I love her.

One evening in late September 1911, he met her outside the British Museum 'as she sailed from the darkness of the area… into the light of the lamps. I believe I felt something more like flesh and blood love for her than I have ever done before.' She was just saying farewell to a Professor who she used to study under in Chicago and who was writing a History of Religion. She told Freeman that she normally had her evening meal with him and he apparently looked at the Professor 'very jealously' for he knew his Juliet was going out with another man. (This Professor was James T. Shotwell, who shared Juliet's interest in socialism. He played an instrumental role in the creation of the international Labour Organisation in the USA in 1919 and in 1952 was nominated for the Nobel Peace Prize).

Whether from his inexperience, youthful innocence or the naive way he coped with relationships, the next few pages of Freeman's diary deal with his agonising over whether Juliet had feelings for him or not. He was strikingly unsure about what love is or what it feels like, what meaning his long conversations with Juliet might have, and 'whether there's any sex feelings in her liking for me' which he doubted he would ever discover without asking 'a point-blank question.' Perhaps as a consequence of his previous painful experience with Winifred, AJF remained reluctant to overtly express his feelings to Juliet, for fear she should 'curl up into her shell.' He indulged in imagining how it would be to introduce her to his family and friends:

> What a Goddess she is compared with my brothers' harmless wives. How she will annoy all of my circle. It will be most glorious to hear her talking to them, as she did to me last night, about the need for bloodshed and revolution and war in order that labour might get its rights! And she'll talk about sexual questions and prostitution… Oh my dear Joan how you will stir them up.

He also considered their differing religious and spiritual perspectives and how, in contrast to him, she prioritised the material problems of society above spiritual questions. Juliet disliked the socialism of the Fabian Society and she wanted this bourgeois society shattered and had 'a vague Marxian faith that utopia will arise from the ashes. There is something of Rousseau in her talk about returning to the simple life.'

Freeman tells us that after completing her DSc work, which would be in the spring of 1912, Juliet aspired to earn a living from journalism. Another day they met at Shearer's for lunch and afterwards he walked with her to the British Museum and presented her with two books on British history and offered to help her with her 'thesis on the Chartists', which she politely declined because she 'would have nothing ready before Christmas.'

At this point in their relationship Freeman was, once again, seriously thinking about proposing to her but hesitated because he wanted to wait until they knew each other better now that she had decided to stay in England. It was more sensible 'to leave this in the hands of Fate and await the inspiration of the moment', and so he turned to Florence Huntley's *Harmonics of Evolution* for inspiration and to test whether he and Juliet were compatible.

Further correspondence ensued, mainly dealing with the publication of her paper. On Saturday September 14th they met in the basement parlour of her lodgings at 91, Gower Street, where she read him her paper whilst he listened and made suggestions. They were joined later for tea by Miss Cummings, Juliet's friend, to talk about the English and the philosophy of Shaw's *Man and Superman*. Juliet told Freeman that she was intending to extend her stay in England for another two years to spend more time on her thesis, despite the fact that she couldn't stand her supervisor Graham Wallas (1858-1932) and her only worry was that she had to work with him.[22]

In early November 1911 Freeman was in Penarth, when he wrote a letter finally telling Juliet how he felt about her. The full contents of the letter he wrote to her remain unknown, but he tells us that he made 'the staggering statement that "I think I love you more than anyone else I know"'. Juliet responded with some remarks on philosophical questions addressed by Freeman but then she said that:

> I find you a very nice sort of person as you are and I am not going to spoil my enjoyment of your individuality by trying to make you something different. But I think that experience will change your point of view before you die.

This response confused him and he wondered what it all meant, thinking it might be a cold and calculated answer to his 'staggering statement… it is rather odd that she should, apparently, go out of her way to make a remark of this sort, at variance with what she has said before.' Juliet, he confessed, was as sensitive and intuitive as other women so she must suspect that he was 'in love with her.' Freeman even wondered if she thought that 'all the pretty things I say to her are the exuberance of my boyishness.'

On his return from Penarth they met upstairs in the Lyceum for tea and from the diary entries for that day it is obvious that his deep and passionate feelings for her remained undiminished:

> Oh! It was so beautiful! My darling Joan I wish I could have put my arms around you! I'm afraid my old feeling of intellectual admiration is beginning to transform itself into passionate love… she was

most beautifully dressed in brown and wore a brown hat... her beauty lies not so much in physical as in spiritual qualities. There's a mysticism, a depth, a deepness in her physiognomy that haunts and lures you. I sat for three hours scarcely taking my eyes off her face and it was a feast of spiritual beauty such as I have rarely had... we had a delicious talk... the most intimate talk I have had with her and never before have we drawn so close together.

Arnold suggested that they met more regularly or at least every week, but she replied that she scarcely went out at all, 'that she lived a hermit sort of life', and she was not in good health as she was having morphine injections; but what really prevented her from socialising more is that she loathed English people. In reality, it is likely she was lying about her hermetic existence as she was already seeing another man whom she later married. They spent the remainder of the day together and had dinner at a local restaurant where the conversation turned to the inevitable subject of religion, but also prostitution, Sean Williams, Joan of Arc and Socialism. The diary entry for that day finished with him comparing Juliet with the other 'love' in his life, with Juliet as if favourite, being:

So full of ideas, of imagination, of spirit, of mystery. I could be with Joan through eternity and never cease to wonder at the treasures of her soul. I am beginning to pray to God that she may be the companion marked out for me from the beginning of the world.

While lecturing for the Theosophical Society AJF received a letter from Juliet confirming that her paper would be ready for the volume in progress and she mentioned a picture that Arnold sent her of Joan of Arc:

Your very charming remembrance came yesterday and I have put it in a sort of shrine on the top of my wardrobe. It is a very beautiful thing and I shall always take much pleasure in it. But I must assure you I am not at all the Joan type. Firstly I am too democratic. These medieval saints were fearful snobs and aristocrats. I think there is a new kind of modern saint who has the courage to admit that he isn't that much different from the rest of humanity and may not set the world on fire or lead a crusade but has the true fortitude of resignation. He resigns himself to insignificance. That's the only kind of saint I am. But your Joan is an interesting and beautiful relic.

His response to this was disappointment and he wrote a long letter back to her. However, before she received it, she invited him to meet her on the following Monday. This prompted him to think about whether he really loved her, and offered him the opportunity to 'propose to her tentatively', either in a 'fit of impetuosity or merriment'. Eventually her response to his letter arrived, which again reveals further aspects of her character and personality and her insight into Arnold's:

> I do think we ought to do all we can for the world, but I don't think we can do it (like Buddha or some other Asiatic) by shutting ourselves up and gazing at our umbilicus. I think you are on the wrong track with your development idea… the Joan of Arc you sent me is very beautiful… it reminds me of your kindness in sending it. But I didn't look upon it as an exemplar. Each age has its own type of special leader… Forgive my vehemence. I am trying to shake you out of yourself a bit – to instil relativism in place of the absolutist point of view which dominates you. But you'll come out all right. By the end of your life you will find that this saint business doesn't work in this modern world… and human personality and moral ideals are dynamic as well as mere economic forces… please take this letter as a great compliment. I very seldom take the trouble to abuse people but perhaps the game is worth the candle here.

This letter did not appear to annoy or irritate him and they continued to exchange letters and meet at frequent intervals for serious, intimate and playful conversations. If Freeman's accounts of their meetings are accurate, then their relationship, at least from his perspective, was full of potential. As he put it, 'she does nothing to encourage me, but on the other hand she never does anything to snub me.'

At Christmas 1911 she sent him *The Little Flowers of St. Francis*, with the following written in the flyleaf: 'To a Saint from a Sinner.' In an accompanying letter, obviously directed towards Arnold she wrote that: 'I hope you will like the little book about St. Francis which I love. Everything about him is pervaded by the charming simplicity of his character and as you know, I am a great admirer of his…'

And then with reference to a lecture he was giving at the Lyceum Club on January 31st she remarked that she was looking forward very much to hearing him as he has such a 'splendid spirit. If you'd only concentrate it in the right thing, I just leave one thought with you. One doesn't have to be religious to be spiritual and lead the world to an appreciation of spiritual values.'

Freeman closed his 1911 diary entries with a reference to 'the one problem in my life that I cannot solve by my own efforts: the problem as to whose solution I am in the uttermost perplexity.' This problem was Juliet because he had no idea of where their relationship was going; by the end of next year, he might have 'cooled off' or proposed to her and been refused. As he put it, 'any one of these possibilities might easily become an actuality.'

Juliet attended his address at the Lyceum Club, where a lady got up at the end and said it was one of the best speeches she had ever attended. This turned out to be Mrs Havelock-Ellis to whom Freeman had given a copy of the *Harmonics of Evolution* and had been invited to visit. Afterwards Juliet, Sean Williams and he had dinner at Sean's house, and he learned that Juliet could also paint. He received a note from her afterwards telling him that he 'spoke wonderfully well… you are a little apt to idealise, which in itself is a splendid thing, if only other people were idealists as well.'

Nearly four weeks passed before he heard from Juliet again and she told him she was still struggling with her paper for the *Seasonal Trades* volume. But she also told him that:

> I'm going to Oxford for a year to write about women and work. I am tired of fooling around with Graham Wallas. He's such a poor, stupid, obstinate old wretch. I'll write my thesis at Oxford and take my PhD in America at Columbia.

They met again on Sunday January 27th for lunch with Sean Williams at a restaurant in Piccadilly. After talking a little about sex and marriage

Freeman wondered whether she was in love with him but thought not. They walked to the underground and there parted. Freeman remembered how he felt on that day:

> It looks as if our lives part too… one never knows. I am prepared to believe anything of the future… all I am sure of, for the present, is I am going to shake her as a matrimonial possibility, out of the web of my thought.

Failing to shake her from his thoughts, later that evening during a three hour wait in the queue for a showing of Oedipus Rex, he reflected whether it was time to tell her that he loved her and write her a letter to propose a marriage five years hence. 'Oh, for a woman like Joan to love me.'

He did write her the letter knowing that all was lost with her but asking for sympathy and friendship. He copied her response out in full in the diary and this constitutes the final word he says about her except for an occasional reference:

> Dear Arnold,
>
> You are a funny boy and a naughty one, both of which statements you will agree with, I am sure, by the time I finish this letter. You've probably forgotten by this time all that your last letter was about and my answer may therefore not hit the mark – but here goes. Let me disabuse you firstly, of the illusion that you were ever in love with me or anywhere near it. (Not that it is a very powerful hallucination apparently). If a man is not sure if he loves a woman, he may be quite sure that he does not. Which Shavianism seems to suit your case exactly! No indeed, my dear Arnold, if you were in love with me you would know it. Perhaps you just thought you ought to be – that I was the sort of person – not unintelligent, not hideous etc. and your nervousness came from the consciousness that despite what you ought to have been, you weren't. That's where your dutiful conscience made you miserable. And that's why you're funny. And am I the sort of person to be devoted to from a sense of duty. Fie upon you, Arnold Freeman! Save those noble motives for some

ethereal green-clad Fabian. That's the sort of person one marries (under protest) at the age of 30 or 40 after all attempts at escape have failed. As for me, if I haven't married by 30 (or 80!), it would have been because I didn't believe in marriage (but I do) and should not then change my mind.

She continues by saying she is awfully glad he wrote the letter as 'it has cleared the air wonderfully… and now we can settle down to a peaceful Platonic interest in each others lives where he can tell her all his affairs including the loving ones and when he reaches 60 he may begin to understand his affectionate Godmother, if by then you've not gone blind stargazing.' This was the final letter he received from Juliet and their conversation after the meal in Piccadilly was probably the last time they met.

Juliet was for Freeman the 'ideal woman' who taught him many important truths, so he didn't regret that their relationship ended as its intimacy had made it 'a thousand times worthwhile'. He preserved his freedom and like all his previous relationships, thought he had gained 'valuable experience from each encounter', despite the fact that he was convinced that he'd never experienced love. The following information about Juliet's subsequent life is taken from Denise Lynn's book: *Where Is Juliet Stuart Poyntz?: Gender, Spycraft, and Anti-Stalinism in the Early Cold War (Culture and Politics in the Cold War and Beyond 2021)*.

On October 8th 1913, Poyntz married Dr Friedrich Franz Ludwig Glaser, a communist and attaché at the German consulate in New York, who she met while working as a librarian at the LSE. She kept this relationship secret probably because when she met Glaser he was already married with two children. Even some of Juliet's closest friends were unaware that she had married and around this time she probably returned to the USA.

In 1914 she began working with the Socialist Party's Rand School of Social Science and in 1915 she conducted a study for the Massachusetts Minimum Wage Commission and the Chamber of Commerce on solutions to unemployment. Probably based on her studies in England with Webb and Freeman, she argued that part of the problem for working people was seasonal employment or half-time employment. A solution to this she thought was to guarantee employees a living wage throughout the year. In 1916 Juliet became the first director of the newly created Organization and Education Department of the Ladies' Waist and Dressmakers' Union Local 25 where she developed a programme of adult labour education, organized academic lectures and organized dancing and recreation classes. She was so successful in this that eventually she was offered the position of Education Director of the International Ladies' Garment Workers' Union.

Juliet was also one of the founding members of the Communist Party of America. Throughout the 1920s Poyntz was a leading American communist and in 1934 left the American Branch of the Communist Party to join the Soviet underground, recruiting German and Italian students attending Columbia University to persuade them to return to their home country to work in the anti-fascist underground. She also made several secret trips to the Soviet Union. In 1937 she disappeared after leaving the American Woman's Association Clubhouse at 353 West 57th Street in Manhattan, New York City and was never seen again. It is suspected that Soviet agents assassinated her. Her disappearance and suspected murder occurred at a time of disillusionment among American radicals on the political left and it is suggested that Juliet began to embrace anti-communism and wanted to 'get out' which led to her murder.

Nora White

It was on Tuesday 20th June 1911, on Elsie's wedding day, that Freeman first met his future wife Nora White. There is a particularly long entry in the diary which he wrote a few days later, on his first day in Hannover.

> After the speaking I went up to Miss Nora White and began a conversation with her which was continued for long periods during the rest of the day. She was apparently thought to be the prettiest young lady present, so I was lucky to see so much of her… at my suggestion we discussed Socialism, Votes for Women, Vegetarianism – in fact everything… we talked of psychical research. She thinks nothing can be proved of the fact of a future life by a science of this sort. I did not

tell her I was staking my life on the question. She is, as she described herself rather old-fashioned in her ideas; goes to church; but refused to be classed as an adherent of any of the political parties; does not believe in my views about the position of women… she is one of the most natural unspoilt creatures I ever remember meeting.

He also saw her as 'another possible convert' to the school of TK but thought 'she and I will become chums', and nothing more. As far as her politics were concerned, he thought of her less as a Joan of Arc and more as a 'a friend worth having.' The next reference to Nora is on February 17th, 1912, when he and the twins spent an evening at her home playing games. A month later he refers to her as 'The Angel' when they attended a lecture by a Professor Barrett on 'Swedenborg's Philosophy in the Light of Modern Science'. They travelled home on the top of the bus where she asked 'the inevitable question' of whether he was continuing his studies. He 'explained lamely' what he was doing, and they ended up having a most enjoyable conversation. 'She is a most sweet lovable creature.' A few days later, he spent the day in Epping Forest with the twins, Nora and her sister Florence, with the evening spent playing a game called Crimes. At this point AJF felt confident enough to send her a copy of TK's *The Great Work* which she began to study.

By June 1912 it seems as though Nora and Arnold were in a formal platonic relationship. He met her at the Reservoir where she told him that she had read TK's book and gave him 'a long disquisition on what she felt about it.' He described her attitude as 'broadly that the revelation of Jesus Christ is sufficient… and believed in the possibility of the existence of the Great School, occult powers etc.' He decided she had some 'first rate qualities' but was doubtful whether they would sympathise with each other on the 'mental plane.' Dolly told him before the meeting that she was trying to 'hook' him and he felt very nervous about it as he didn't love her. Freeman reveals that he had a warm corner in his heart for her for a long time, but 'this has come rather suddenly' as he didn't realise she had feelings for him. He remained unsure, reflecting wryly of himself, 'I am the biggest fool in Christendom in all matters of this sort.'

Nora also took an avid interest in Freeman's work on the Prevention of Destitution, which gave him 'a strong impression of cooperative interest' in his life. In other words, it no longer seemed as obvious that marriage would inhibit his work. However, Freeman worried that her strength of character would 'prevent her yielding to my revolutionary or missionary efforts,' thus creating friction between his 'ideas and objectionable qualities and her somewhat conventional and fixed views of life.' Despite these doubts he genuinely liked her, finding her beautiful, healthy, happy, pure, brave, sweet, well educated, and just the sort of wife he wanted. 'An infinitely better sort of character' than he and a far better girl than any of his brothers had married. Freeman eventually admitted that if she continued to smile on him, he would probably fall in love with her and he would be content if that happened.

This was the time in his life when he was making important decisions about his future career; whether to teach, embark on the research fellowship at Woodbrooke or take up the offer of vice principal at Ruskin College. In the context of this, Freeman feared Nora might prevent him from making the right choices, and he considered ending it all with her because he did not love her. On the other hand, he often longed for her and came to realise what a splendid wife she would make. 'I feel that if I do not marry Nora, I will marry no one. What a queer position to be in!'

A few days later, a big change in his emotional life can be seen in his diary, as he realised his love for Nora had been growing steadily and referred to her as 'a divine being, I continually think of her'. In comparison to the other women in his life with whom he had been 'more or less in love', Nora had more good looks than all of them put together, though she had less of an intellectual sense of humour. With her splendid education and practical common sense, Freeman came to believe in the Platonic theory of love, that 'she will supply what is lacking in me.' The next few pages in the diary are laid out like an audit of all the things they have in common and all the skills and qualities they don't share, as if he were still making up his mind. Importantly, on religion they differed, but shared in 'the fundamentals of it'. Nora was also anxious to ameliorate social conditions and believed sufficiently in occultism 'to allow our talking about it together.' He remained anxious that she should accept his commitment to TK's work.

On a walk through Finsbury Park he convinced Nora that he intended to become a respectable member of society, earn a decent living and 'tell people that henceforward I am going to give up my wild ways and wear the white flower of a blameless life'. Writing in the diary after this walk he dreamt of the perfect romantic and harmonious life with her in a country cottage. Nora in the 'kitchen cooking and my coming to sneak a cake… arguing in the morning, lazing in the afternoon, going deep and reverent in the evening and speaking of love under the stars'. A family was also important for Arnold. 'What magnificent children they will be, strong and beautiful and intelligent… I hope the first will be a girl and the next a boy'.

A week later everything changed. AJF's impatience temporarily deflated his longings for Nora. After another walk with her, instead of the expected increase and intensification of his love for her, he felt only 'half in love with her'. With some degree of self-knowledge, he recognised the problem was the 'waiting' and he feared they might get as far as an engagement only to find they were not suited. He agonised over the question of whether she really was his ideal. 'Sometimes I have said Yes… at other times I have felt doubtful and wondered for what I really do like her'. Such prevarication was not unusual in his relationships, and this could be put down to his problem with commitment. Another factor that could have led to his hesitancy was his discovery that because of the radicalism of her father, Nora became an anti-radical and revealed she would never be a socialist. In the end this didn't deter Freeman as he was eager to find out if she really loved him and longed for her to say so, as it would free him from his uncertainty. This didn't happen. After a long conversation AJF wrote that his 'feeling with it all is that never once did I get down to those depths of the sort that ought to be stirred if a man and woman are really in love.' However, in this cloud of uncertainty and insecurity he still lived in hope that they may 'drift into an understanding… I would give all the world if Puck would this night sprinkle a few drops of Love-In-Idleness over my sleeping eyes and show me her first of all creatures next morning… well I can only hope and pray!'

Nora White as a young woman in London, aged about 21.

Freeman's relationship with Nora is a particularly good example of him losing all sense of proportion and over-dramatizing his emotional response when he reflects on his meetings with her. At this relatively earlier stage in their relationship several pages of the diary are filled with an agonising outpouring of whether he loves her. One entry reads:

> Yes there is no doubt I am in love with her. And I have a feeling that it will grow and that I shall get silly and that she will be able to twist me around her finger. Well it will probably do me good. I don't care how madly I fall in love with her. I've had the agnostic and dispassionate phase of love for her... now let passion sweep my being.

He rarely considered whether his feelings were reciprocated or whether she was even interested in pursuing a relationship based on the assumption that it would end in marriage. After making these entries he received two letters from her about changing the arrangements they made for future meetings. Both were addressed to Mr Freeman; the first one was signed 'Yours sincerely' and the second 'Your loyal friend Nora White'. The tone and wording of both letters were very formal, objective and even slightly cool. He said of the first letter that it made him feel rather dazed and tremulous with mixed feelings about it and he kept thinking there was a battle going on 'in me between the rational and irrational. The rational struggled for life.' The second letter referred to a discussion they had had on their favourite bench in Finsbury Park where they disagreed on some fundamental issues especially his work and unwavering interest in the work of TK. In summary Nora writes:

> At present you are honourably bound by an ideal and I would rather have you stick to it, in fact I should despise you if you didn't, so long as it remains your ideal... it does not in anyway narrow my sympathy or prevent me from understanding. I might just as well say that I couldn't air my views when I know quite well that you are antagonistic to them... I can't come on Monday and I can't see you again yet.

At Nora's instigation they did, however, meet again to attend the 1912 Shakespeare Exhibition at Earl's Court. They sat down to talk and 'within five minutes I had learned with an astonishment, which I did not betray, that she not only was not fond of me but never had been – in the romantic sense.' He wrote that her impression of him was that he was resolved not to get married and would never dream of such a thing. Their relationship, as far as Nora was concerned, was based purely on friendship accompanied by the notion that she could perhaps help him in one way or another with his work.

This meeting convinced Freeman that his relationship with Nora would remain on a friendly basis and she would be his 'ideal comrade,' although he felt as though he had been a fool, 'I am a fool and a weakling. And yet I am not at all sorry that this has happened. I love Nora more now than ever I did before. I have lost a wife but won a friend.' He tells us that he felt a sinking feeling over it all, but on the whole he felt relieved that his life was now free, 'now at last all is cleared up and work will take its place'.

A month later he received an unexpected letter from Nora. 'How strangely things work out' he declared in response to this, 'I really did think that was the end of the romance of Arnold and Nora.' In the letter Nora stated that she 'could have cared tremendously if I had wanted it' and suggested that if he still loved her in a year's time then she would be happy for him to 'come and ask me to come into your life and we will work together for the ideal that is before us both.' Freeman was dumbfounded, overjoyed and amazed and readily agreed to wait a year 'to get clear and make certain; and we are both free to do as we will till then.' Following this revelation from Nora, they met frequently to discuss their future together, but decided to postpone an engagement until Arnold's future was more secure.

Throughout 1912 their relationship had its difficult moments largely due to Arnold's fear of commitment and his pompous attitude whenever anyone criticised his relationship to TK. Just before Christmas this came to a climax after meeting Nora's sister Florence and two friends in Southend. He notes his frustration in his diary:

> I came home feeling fearfully irritated… this is partly my diabolical hatred of having to settle down and make myself agreeable and play cards (which I hate) and kiss babies (whom I hate).

He also says one other 'great cause' of his disappointments, 'an old one of long standing', was Nora's lack of sympathy with TK's ideas. He was sick and very hurt of hearing people telling him that nothing good would come out of his work with TK, and he wished Nora would appreciate Bernard Shaw, and become 'really alive to the meaning of TK's work'. He did, however, attempt to adopt a philosophical view to his relationship 'problems' and to see the positive side of it by looking at Nora's skills and qualities. On Boxing Day, he travelled to Southend to meet her where they agreed they would have 'lovers' quarrels'; an agreement which appears to have temporarily solved the problem because he went there again on the following Monday when they shared their 'first kiss' and got 'closer and closer and closer' to each other. In his yearly 1912 reflection he wrote that Nora:

> Is everything to me, more than any TK or any sort of Saviour or God. To work for her and be with her seem often to be all the aspirations I have in life. I have been very agnostic about her in the past, even of late, for a flash sometimes.

He goes on to say that he often felt they were not really suited but 'those feelings become more and more impossible.' He wanted her and only her, 'not only in this life but in all the lives that stretch ahead of us.'

AJF cultivated his relationship with Nora over the next couple of years and she was also with him, when she was not working, at Birmingham during his research into *Boy Life and Labour*. She even wrote a small part of the book and they eventually married in 1914. What is remarkable about his relationships with Juliet and Nora is his constant effort to 'convert' them to the writings of the American Guru TK, about whom we will learn more in chapter six, but before his 'meeting' with TK, he continued his path 'seeking for the spirit' by delving into spiritualism, psychical research, automatic writing and embracing the ideas of the Theosophical Society.

Chapter Five
Spiritualism and Theosophy

Seeking the Spirit

Two diary entries from 1905 offer us the first clues to the nineteen-year-old Freeman's belief in the afterlife and interest in spiritualism. Around this time, he was reading William Thomas Stead's *Letters from Julia*, a famous work on spiritualism that was, according to Stead, a record of conversations communicated by means of automatic writing between him and the deceased American journalist, Julia Amis. Further to this, Freeman records discussing automatic writing with Mrs Vivian and friends on a visit to Bradford the same year. He noted afterwards how reassuring he found this; that it helped convince him of the 'evolving spirit', of life after death, 'the truth of automatic writing', and how he felt 'less fearful of death'.

The Mesmerising Literature

Freeman's reading of the *Letters from Julia* in 1905 awakened in him an interest in the 'esoteric' and was a starting point on his path of occult discovery. Whilst at Oxford he had taken a brief interest in personal magnetism when he'd met a certain student from New Zealand. It wasn't until 1907, when he attended a lecture at 'the Guild by Bennett on the Society for Psychical Research' (SPR), that we find him taking a more serious interest in the spirit world. This lecture was given by Edward Trusted Bennett (1831-1908), sometime secretary of the SPR and author of books on automatic writing, psychic phenomena and spiritualism. His most famous work was *The Society for Psychical Research: Its Rise, Progress and Sketch of its Works* (1903). Freeman thought his lecture was fascinating and notes that they had 'many photos of spirits… instances of telepathy were abundant and also instances of spirit manifestations.' The evidence of 'continuity of existence', he wrote, 'cannot be overrated. It will make people believe in a real hell and a real heaven.' He immediately reached out to the SPR for further information.

The Society for Psychical Research was founded in 1882 with the purpose of investigating mesmeric, psychical and 'spiritualist' phenomena in a purely scientific way.[23] The society's foundation coincided with the development of widespread belief in supernatural forces and the occult, and the SPR is credited with having had a big influence on the late Victorian Gothic revival. Occult, supernatural and spiritualist themes also influenced other forms of popular culture such as novels, stage plays and works of non-fiction. Freeman, for example, was reading 'occult' literature, including Katherine Bates's book *Seen and Unseen* which was a personal record of her psychic experiences. This lead AJF to come to the conclusion that 'this little earth body is a mere temporary shelter for something infinitely greater than our familiar little intelligence.' His reading of Bates's book helped confirm his nascent belief in psychic phenomena and, on the strength of that, he resolved to read Frederick Henry William Myers' (1843-1901) book *Human Personality and Its Survival of Bodily Death*.

Freeman was also very familiar and made notes on Mabel Collins' book, *Light on the Path*, a popular esoteric text which has gone through numerous editions since its first publication in 1885. He was also reading the well-known Victorian novel *Zanoni* published in 1842, written by Edward Bulwer-Lytton which tells the story of Zanoni who possessed occult powers and knew the secret of eternal life. From his reading of occult and spiritualist literature Freeman began to believe that human beings possess higher faculties of perception, the development of which could eventually lead to 'initiation', insight into spiritual worlds and eventually 'Mastership'.

Mabel Collins's book was a key Theosophical text for inner development and encouraged those who hoped for spiritual self-transformation. Freeman found her work 'wonderful', and committed himself to taking on a journey of spiritual development:

At the present I must aim at nothing except the perfection of my character through love… to think of each soul as individual and vital, not as a mere dash of paint on the scenery of my life… I must perfect my character that I may be worthy for the deeper truths when the time comes. I must learn Sympathy, Fearlessness, Humility, self-control, indifference. I must learn that: *Before the voice can speak in the presence of the Masters, it must have lost the power to wound.*

Mabel Collins's book, from which the final sentence is copied, obviously made an impression on him, and he claimed that it increased his 'yearning for fuller knowledge and power'.

The widely held supernatural beliefs of the late Victorian and early Edwardian period included spiritualism, astral travel, ritual magic, and a belief in reincarnation. Like many individuals at this time, Freeman felt that the orthodox Christian Church had failed to fill the need for sacramental experiences (the Victorian Crisis of Faith) and had a great desire to explore beliefs beyond the boundaries of orthodox religion. For example, his belief in the possibility of life beyond death became grounded in reality for him as he gazed at his grandmother's corpse:

I have never seen her look as beautiful in life. All her wrinkles were smoothed out. Her face was firm and peaceful. She looked exactly as if she were carved in marble… as I looked on her that night I felt more strongly than ever the certainty of a life after death. The idea of *that* being the end seemed absurd and impossible.

Julia's Bureau

William Thomas Stead's activities as a spiritualist and his fame as a controversial journalist and activist in this period, made a small but significant contribution to the spread of supernatural ideas at the turn of the 20th century.[24] His journal *Borderlands*, despite only being in circulation for four years, found a wide readership and contained reports and articles on a variety of subjects including astrology, séances and psychical research. In April 1909, Stead opened 'Julia's Bureau' at Mowbray House,

Norfolk Street, London, for the purpose of bridging the gap between the living and the dead, and séances were held with some of the leading mediums of the day. He called it the *Bureau* 'because it is in effect an office with a clerical staff, archives and the ordinary machinery of a Bureau.' Its business, however, was 'strictly limited to one thing, namely, to endeavour to put into communication those who are sorrowing for their beloved dead with the spirits of those whose bodies have been laid to rest in the earth.'[25]

AJF was a regular visitor to Julia's Bureau, sometimes accompanied by his mother. On his first visit Stead came out to shake his hand. He described Stead's manner as 'brusque, but he makes you feel that there is a large warm heart under his rugged exterior.' His reason for visiting was that he wished to help out and during some of the séances he took notes for those who were attending. On the visit with his mother, Vango, one of the mediums 'told mother some remarkable details about Dad's illness and death bed and gave both of us a good description of Dad.' On another occasion he was overjoyed to be invited to attend a materialising séance where a spirit takes on a physical form. He described one séance as follows:

> I saw one of the spirits very closely. She came within about a foot of me and I saw the features quite plainly. As far as I could see she had no proper legs, all her lower part was filmy white stuff that was translucent. Often a spirit would sink down and half disappear before my eyes.

Another time Johnson, one of the psychics, attempted to hypnotise him and placed his head on one chair and feet on another where he remained mesmerised for about two minutes. Afterwards he visited Johnson at his flat in 42, Bedford Court Mansions, who told him they were meant to help each other as they were acquainted in a previous incarnation. He also advised Freeman not to develop his psychic powers 'but to go on with my ordinary work and let things take their course.' Freeman's visits to the Bureau convinced him 'of the fact of a future life... I think I must reckon this the most wonderful day of my life.' Later, however, he notes that he was 'not willing to say as yet' whether he was 'a believer in any forms of belief,

Christian Science, Materialist or Theosophist. I incline most to Theosophy but I must wait for "More Light! More Light!"'

Stead was well known for holding interviews with deceased statesmen. Freeman reports on a transcript of one read out by Stead:

> The great incident of the week has been a reputed interview between Stead and the spirit of Gladstone on the budget. Stead read us the last passage of an unpublished automatic letter from W.E.G. which was certainly in the old man's vein. I suggested that Julia's Bureau would soon be directing the affairs of the Empire, but he said No! Julia did not like interfering in worldly affairs.

Stead often predicted that he would either die by lynching or drowning, a prophecy that came true when he drowned at sea in the Titanic disaster on 15th of April 1912, while travelling to speak on world peace at the Great Men and Religions conference in New York City that was scheduled to take place on 22nd April.

A Struggling Soul, Christian Science and Theosophy

During his exploration of the occult sciences and 'alternative religions', Freeman discovered Mary Baker Eddy's (1821-1910) Christian Science which he thought would help him to develop his psychic or 'super-normal powers'. He believed that to achieve this would require him to devote several hours a day to the study of Christian Science. The main theme in Eddy's book *Science and Health* is, however, the argument that sickness is an illusion, and a practicing Christian Scientist, by living according to the spiritual laws of God and by taking the teachings of Jesus as an example, would experience a 'more real and tangible healing and regeneration' quite naturally. There is no specific reference to a strict course of spiritual development with its associated spiritual exercises such as one might find in the works of other spiritual teachers, especially Theosophists.

The diaries indicate that Freeman's interest in Christian Science led him to attend testimonial meetings in Oxford and in London with his brother Peter and to give Eddy's *Science and Health* a cursory read.

Eventually Freeman realised that he needed to find a balance between his academic work and his spiritual striving. While he did once declare that he was 'nine-tenths Christian Scientist', his diaries suggest that he remained ambivalent about it. For instance, he didn't like how the other Christian Scientists 'worshipped' Mrs Eddy, as he thought this restricted the development of their individualism and the members needed to disengage themselves from her, as much of what she said was 'jargon'. Thus, Freeman's foray into Christian Science was fairly short-lived, but the underlying questions that had compelled him to seek answers in spiritualism in the first place had not gone away.

The first months of 1909 were difficult for AJF as he was questioning his personal religion, nursing fears about his future in Oxford, revolting against democracy, hating his study of economics and feeling a great aching for the sorrow of the world: 'all these questions have been ever crowding in upon my brain and together they have brought to me that most awful of conditions – a disbelief in myself.' He felt as though he had turned 'from old ideas to new ones... in fact all my questionings end in the question of questions: What is Truth?'

As we have seen, in his search for truth, Freeman embraced many different religious, philosophical and spiritual teachings. Indeed, his mother once accused him of changing his religion on a daily basis, which frustrated Arnold, as his protean approach to spiritual and religious belief caused further friction in the family. His mother's accusation might give rise to the impression that Freeman imbibed a new philosophy or theology, cherished it for a short time, only to discard it when it didn't meet his intellectual or emotional needs anymore. While it is true that his practical approach in finding answers to life's greatest questions caused him to search through a broad range of beliefs, there was an underlying and unifying intention behind his actions. It was never out of curiosity but out of a deeper impulse to build a 'social religion' that he explored so widely; he sought a set of beliefs that would be 'a religion for the individual and a religion for society.' On leaving Oxford we know that many of his old ideals had been quashed and he left his 'old faith' behind him. He wanted to build a strong new religion that he thought would be a synthesis of all the many different religious beliefs and philosophies of life that he had assimilated over the years since leaving school.

It is therefore not surprising that Freeman's interest also turned to Theosophy and the Theosophical Society, originally founded by Helena Petrovna Blavatsky (1831-1891) and Colonel Henry Steel Olcott (1832-1907) in New York in 1875. Theosophy contributed greatly to the 'occult revival' at the turn of the twentieth century.[26] Blavatsky and her two major publications, and later Annie Besant (1847-1933), were most influential in the promotion of its spiritual philosophy. Blavatsky's *Isis Unveiled* (1877) and *The Secret Doctrine* (2 vols. 1888) were fundamental to the spread of occult ideas and some of what we know as 'New Age' comes out of Theosophy's spiritual philosophy. It has been suggested that Blavatsky made esotericism part of mainstream culture and revealed long hidden spiritual teachings to make them available for all individuals irrespective of age, race or cultural background. Annie Besant took over the Presidency of the Society in 1907 after a career as a social and women's rights activist, among other things. It was under her leadership that the Society began preparing the world for the coming of the 'World Teacher', for his arrival on Earth in the near future.

The first mention of Theosophy in Arnold's diaries relates how his piano teacher Ehrenmayer 'unfolded to him his belief' in Theosophy and defended it with 'considerable reasonableness.' It was on May 14th, 1909, that AJF attended his first theosophical lecture in London together with his brother Peter. Annie Besant gave the lecture as she was on a world tour, having given a series of fifteen lectures on The Changing World at Queen's Hall, London, before attending the Annual Theosophical Convention of Great Britain and Ireland. This was two months after Charles Leadbeater 'discovered' the young boy Krishnamurti on the beach of the Theosophical headquarters in Adyar, India, who they intended to present to the world as a high initiate and future vehicle for the second coming of Christ himself. Freeman notes that Besant spoke about a new wave of thought breaking through and another silently forming behind it and revealed that 'somewhere was a Messiah who would declare the Gospel'. A few days later he heard her again, lecturing on *The Coming Race*.

On Monday July 5th, 1909, Freeman visited Besant and afterwards wrote a positive description of her, in stark contrast to his impression of her character when he wrote about her again some twelve years later. His first thoughts were as follows:

> I was much struck by her gentleness and sweetness of manner. She is certain that the Christ is coming soon – probably as far as I could gather, in the next thirty years, certainly in my lifetime if I live to threescore years and ten. I said I wished she were as young as I so that she could see Him and she replied that she would be a younger soul than I was then. She advised me to go on studying economics and theosophy for the next few years. She felt that reform was coming from the self-sacrifice of the rich rather than from the uprising of the poor.

He pressed her particularly hard on the point of whether they lived in the 'growing goodness of the times'. Besant thought that the age of materialism had passed, and the spiritual life was deepening. She thought everything was in ferment and that reconstruction must come or else catastrophe.

Both Arnold and Peter attended as many of Besant's lectures as they could and on Sunday June 27th they heard her lecture on the Coming Christ. Freeman was clearly influenced by this as he wrote afterwards that 'the coming of a Great Teacher will soon arise… I know that we are on the eve of the most marvellous changes and discoveries and combinations that the world has ever seen… Mrs Besant urged us to make ready for his coming and I must do so.'

He and Peter also went to hear her lecture on *The Place of Theosophy in the Coming Civilisation* which later became the title of a book published in 1910 containing all fifteen lectures given by her during the months of May, June and July 1909. He seemed very engaged with her ideas; 'I have found the truth in Theosophy. I want nothing better than to serve the Great White Brotherhood and to follow the Christ when He comes, upon whatever path He goes.' He went on to say, having finished reading Besant's autobiography:

Her story is that of one of the noblest souls of whom history gives us a record. I marvel to think of what that woman has endured. Her incredible earnestness in the search for Truth and her wonderful intellectual powers make me feel much surer than I was that in following her lead and joining the Theosophists I have not gone astray.

The Theosophical Society and Annie Besant

During his holiday in August 1909 Freeman then read a selection of theosophical pamphlets that inspired him to join the Theosophical Society, which he did, together with his brother Peter, on September 12th. He joined because by this point, he found that theosophy 'best accords with my spiritual and intellectual needs.' He deepened his knowledge of occultism by attempting to read Samuel Roberts Maxwell's *Unseen Forces and How to Use Them* (1903), where he 'learnt clearly for the first time how thought cures are accomplished'.

He also turned to Oliver Lodge's (1851-1940) *Life and Matter: A Criticism of Professor Haeckel's 'Riddle of the Universe'*, as a reliable guide and 'confirmation of all the views that I am beginning to make my stock in trade'. He trusted Lodge because of his qualifications and expertise in the physical sciences, which led him to see the value in pursuing a course in science himself. Freeman's growing belief in thought transference and levitation was also confirmed by a reading of William James' (1842-1910) *Varieties of Religious Experience*, but the most important book he read at this time and 'the most useful book I have ever read' was *Raja Yoga* (1896) by Swami Vivekananda (1863-1902) as 'the marvels that its author declares possible are such as to put the miracles of the apocryphal gospels to the blush. And yet I believe them possible and possible for me.'

Two years later in May 1911, whilst he and Peter were in Oxford, they went to hear Annie Besant lecture at the Clarendon. Arnold took the opportunity to ask her about putting himself as a pupil under the guru known as 'TK':

She said that she did not know him, that she had just heard his name and went on to warn me against putting myself under some quack teacher who would set me exercises that would undermine brain and body.

Arnold was obviously very disappointed with her answer and Peter then tried to persuade her to come to Cardiff to open the new Theosophical Lodge, which Peter had just founded. She apparently refused and was equally evasive when asked when exactly the Christ was coming, saying that she knew but 'might not tell.' The conversation continued with Arnold trying to persuade her to convert George Bernard Shaw to Theosophy, 'but she did not tell me whether she would do as I said.' The conversation, he records, was less satisfactory than the one he had with her two years prior. 'Mrs Besant seemed more elusive.'

Despite his obvious disappointment, he nevertheless described her physically, in terms more flattering than those found in the media today:

> She looked exceedingly well. She is an ugly woman, rather squat in build; her short-cropped hair is snowy white, her front teeth are broken and deformed and she wears glasses. She looks like an ugly middle-class woman. But what redeems her is her wonderful self-command and beautiful kindliness. And of course, there is something nobler than beauty in her face – there is the soul of beauty.

Back in London, after hearing her lecture on the *Steps in Evolution*, Freeman was inspired to write that she poured 'forth one rolling sentence of eloquence after another, clothed in her robe of white, full of her message, inspired by God, you felt she was more like a Goddess than a woman.' After lunch the next day they attended a 'Theosophical tea party' and met Besant and 'Alcyone' (Krishnamurti). Although Freeman never spoke to him, he recorded that: 'He is young, bashful, dreamy looking and seems to feel rather out of place always. He may be the Coming Christ for all I know!'

To prepare for the Coming Christ Annie Besant founded the Order of the Star of the East in Adyar, India in 1911. Freeman must have attended one of their first meetings in England when on Sunday 10th September 1911 he heard Annie Besant and Krishnamurti give short talks. He noted the following about the latter, to whom he referred to as Alcyone:

Alcyone spoke in somewhat slow-flowing and hesitating English. He said that his 'Master' had told him to come back to England to study at Oxford in two years' time. Then he urged us to live pure lives etc. in preparation for the coming of the Christ.

He was, however, not impressed with the other theosophists who attended. He wrote that 'those people with their bygone costumes, their weird faces, Freaks (like me) are the only word to describe them. Are these truly the heralds of the Star of the East? Are these the wise men and women come to worship him?'

Freeman's involvement with Theosophy, meeting Annie Besant and hearing her lectures, fired his enthusiasm to the extent that he began to fantasise about a utopian future in England. Besant, he noted, believed that new doors were opening for religion, science and art and she firmly rejected the 'worthlessness of all our churches.' There were, she asserted, unmistakeable signs of a mighty change to counter the 'selfishness and sordidness of the huge masses of people'. Inspired by her words, Freeman connected the message to the rising interest in socialism, which he found to be 'a spiritual, unselfish, Christ-like thing, the outcome of the best thought and feeling of which men are capable.' He praised the advance of science, saying that 'Science is proving beyond a doubt that there is a future life and that we can communicate with the next world; that human beings are not material but spiritual, that the great reality is Spirit and not matter, that the human soul has such powers that Jesus did not exaggerate when he said it could move mountains. Utopias are written in sober sincerity as realisable for our children if not for us.'

AJF saw this socialist utopia as a realistic possibility within the next fifty years, and desired to be endowed with miraculous spiritual powers so as to take part in creating it. All he needed to build the Kingdom of Heaven was to persuade a great number of the right sort of people to help him achieve it. It is probably no coincidence that Freeman wrote this after hearing Annie Besant's lecture on *The Coming Race*, where she said:

The coming civilisation which will be one brotherhood and that tends to friendship between nations, all that helps forward the realisation of a common manhood, that will be the characteristic of the coming race. Those who would prepare themselves for the part of that changed type of man must begin building it up in their character, their emotions, their minds today, by meditation, the opening of the consciousness by practise, the training of the life into expressions along higher lines. That race will be the builder of a universal religion, in which sharing what each has of truth will be the only form of missionary effort. That Race will be the builder of a brotherly civilisation, in which the need of every man will be the measure of what he has given to him; in which the power of every man will be the limit of his responsibility.

This extract from the lecture, the last part strongly mimicking the Marxian adage 'from each according to his abilities, to each according to his needs', must have made a deep impression on Freeman because from this point onwards he wrote in his diary that he wished to dedicate his inner life to working towards 'master-ship'.

On Thursday November 3rd, 1911, Freeman visited his brother Peter in Penarth and gave three lectures. 'The Path to Freedom' he delivered to the Cardiff Branch of the Theosophical Society, and to an audience at the Lesser Town Hall in Pontypridd he spoke on 'Theosophy and Social Unrest' and afterwards of 'Theosophy and the Coming of a Great Teacher'. The next day, while having lunch with Peter at the Factory, they discussed the idea of the coming of the Christ but Arnold remained sceptical and refused to take it on the trust of Annie Besant alone, though he did concede that she founded the Order of the Star of the East specifically in preparation for this event. On Monday November 7th he lectured at Barry on the recently published government 'Minority Report' and at the Adult School at Newport on the 'Prevention of Destitution'. At the end of November at the Hampshire Club House he gave a talk on 'Economic Aspects of Trade Unionism' and later visited a branch of the Fabian Society to give a lecture on 'Religion without Supernaturalism'. Meanwhile he was also busy rehearsing for the *Cheerful Companion* where he played the part of the irascible 'Tory father'. So, his interest in Theosophy had clearly sparked a phase of productivity and confidence for him.

On Saturday 2nd December 1911, Freeman attended a matinee of Macbeth and then travelled down to Brighton and stayed with Madame Jean Delaire, a pseudonym of the French/American science fiction author, essayist and theosophist Pauline Celestine Elisa Touchemolin (1868-1950). On Sunday afternoon he lectured to members of the Theosophical Society on 'The New Science and the Old'. He recorded that he, 'slept in the bed Krishnamurti occupied some months previously. If the Christ comes in his body, I shall feel this to have been a great honour!'

In the following week he gave a series of lectures to the Theosophical Society branches in Petersfield, Portsmouth, Bournemouth and Plymouth. One lecture he recorded was on Reincarnation and Socialism. This burst of lectures, travel, and outward-going energy seems to have been precipitated by Freeman's involvement with the Theosophical Society, and was a consequence both of his natural extroversion, and of the theosophical message of urgent preparation for the imminent return of the Lord. The story of Krishnamurti, who Besant and Leadbeater were grooming to be the new 'World Teacher', is too long to be told here, but it appears that AJF lost interest in the possible return of the 'Lord Maitreya' as he turned to another teacher, a story explored in the next chapter.

Arnold's mother Edith at Carbis Bay, Cornwall.
She lived to be 100.

1950, Arnold, his mother Edith, his son Peter and granddaughter Pearl.

1951, Nora at Clarendon Road, Sheffield. She loved her garden.

1951, Arnold at Clarendon Road, Sheffield in his old dressing gown with photos of his mother and Rudolf Steiner behind him.

1959, Arnold on Marsland Beach, North Devon.

1956, Arnold with his granddaughters, Pearl, Penny and Pam
on the cliff above Marsland Beach, North Devon.

*Late 1960s, Arnold, granddaughter Pearl and her husband Peter
at the bungalow they built in Frogshall Lane, Wymondham.*

Arnold relaxing in his garden.

Chapter Six
The Guru

Finding the Guru

This chapter examines a period in Freeman's life that had a profoundly formative influence on his future, namely his years as a devoted follower of the American guru known as 'TK'. Despite the clear importance of these years in his life, Freeman makes little to no mention of the people or events involved in later biographical writings. This has led some to assume that his involvement with TK was brief, and that the mere suggestion by a fellow student that TK was a charlatan was enough to dissuade Freeman. The truth is somewhat more complicated. For a start, AJF was involved with the works of TK for over six years, and it was more a consequence of his growing maturity and the influence of his wife Nora that Arnold stopped studying the works of TK. By piecing together the evidence, this chapter offers for the first time a detailed account of Freeman's involvement with TK, which began with his older friend Sean Williams, and TK's *The Great Work*.

The Making of a Guru and The Great School

It was in 1909 whilst attending a meeting at Julia's Bureau that Freeman first met Sean Williams, who introduced him to the works of TK, loaning him copies of the guru's works. He remembered the meeting as follows:

> Two or three people were already there and I had a long chat with a Mr Williams who had been to the Bureau in the morning. He is a splendid old chap one of the most refined and finished gentlemen

I have ever met. He said he has always been of a critical nature, (apparently he has written a great deal on scientific subjects) but he found it difficult to resist such evidence as he had heard that morning… this old chap had met Madame Blavatsky and seemed to know everything and everybody. I felt anxious to come in closer touch with him and was delighted when he offered to send me a book called *The Great Work*. It is by an American whom a friend of his met and declared to be the greatest man alive in the world.

This 'greatest man alive' was John Emmet Richardson (1853-1935) also known as the Master TK. Richardson, then a practising attorney, founded The Great School of Natural Science in Stockton, California, in 1884. Allegedly, the inspiration for the founding of the School was Richardson's encounter with a stranger at the Grand Central Hotel in Stockton, who took him to his room and offered him 'Personal Instruction', that enabled him to 'demonstrate the continuity of life beyond the grave'. Thereafter, Richardson commenced on a thirteen-month journey of instruction with this stranger which ended when they both travelled 'out of their physical bodies' to the Central Temple of the Order in Tibet where Richardson was initiated as the 33rd 'member' on 18th August, 1884. Some accounts say that the stranger was an Indian gentleman who introduced himself as *Hoo-Kna-ka*, a representative of the School of the Masters, based in Tibet.

The above account was sourced from Sylvester West's book: *TK and The Great Work in America* (1918), a hostile polemic, published with the intention of undermining Richardson's veracity, his work, methods, publications and, above all, his authenticity as a spiritual teacher.[27] West provides unreferenced evidence to show that he could never have met 'a Hindu as a guest of the Grand Pacific Hotel' as someone of that race and ethnicity (and resident for thirteen months) would not have gone unnoticed. Whether this story is true I leave to the good judgement of readers, and whether Freeman believed it we shall never know. There is no reference in Freeman's diaries to Richardson's personal life or how the Great School was founded. West does, however, reproduce an autobiographical sketch of TK's life which is difficult to verify, but he does say that after the so-called initiation of Richardson as the 33rd member of 'the Order', he and his future wife Florence Huntley founded the Great School of Natural Science which was legally an educational foundation.

Florence Huntley supported Richardson up until her death in 1912. In 1894 they moved to Chicago and in 1907 founded the Indo-American Book Company, which published Huntley's and Richardson's books; the Harmonic Series. They also began the periodical *Life in Action,* to which Freeman purchased a subscription. According to some accounts, Huntley was the brains behind Richardson's entire literary success. She was well educated, trained as a journalist and a talented writer. It is suggested that it was Huntley who edited or even rewrote everything of any merit that TK ever produced. In 1892 she wrote *The Harmonic Series* and *The Dream Child*, and in 1897, *The Harmonics of Evolution*. She edited Richardson's books including *The Great Psychological Crime*, 1903; *The Destructive Principle of Nature in Individual Life*, 1903; and *The Great Work, The Constructive Principle of Nature in Individual Life*, 1907. Richardson, it is argued, wrote nothing after *The Great Work*. They eventually married on January 30th, 1910, but Florence died two years later at home in Oak Park, Illinois, on February 1st, 1912.

The Great School was financed almost solely through the sale of their books and journal and by correspondence courses, but it also received generous donations from individuals such as Herman Hille. Hille (1871-1962) was an organic chemist who, together with the American chemist Albert Coombes Barnes (1872-1951), developed Argyrol, an antiseptic based on silver nitrate protein to resolve local infections in mucous membrane-lined organs, most widely publicized for its efficacy against gonorrhoea infections. It was first made commercially available in 1901 by the Barnes and Hille Chemists Company. Barnes bought out Hille in 1907 for a substantial sum but went on to make millions. Hille went to live in Cook, Chicago, and started his own enterprise. He was naturalized in 1907, and got married to Christina Aronson, a Swedish immigrant. They had a daughter, Mona Wandaniita (1909-2000), while living in Oak Park, Illinois, near Chicago. Hille was already a member of the Theosophical Society and later joined John Richardson to become his ambassador.

Freeman met with Hille in a London hotel in July 1912, where they talked exclusively about TK's *The Great Work*, and this reinforced Freeman's resolve to continue with his spiritual studies. As he said of their meeting, 'If I ever had any doubts about its genuineness he has dispelled them.' Moreover, Freeman was impressed by Hille's financial backing of TK, noting that in 1908 Hille contributed fifty thousand dollars to a Trust Fund for the specific purpose of carrying on 'a beneficent work of education for mankind.'

The Road to 'Mastership'

Jirah Dewey Buck (1838-1916) was also an avid and active supporter of Richardson. He was a physician and a prolific writer on Theosophical subjects and spoke favourably about the Great School. He was also a leading member of the Theosophical Society and was credited by Madame Blavatsky as being instrumental in the spread of the Society and its teachings in America. Buck's favourable attitude towards Richardson, Huntley and the Great School is expressed in his book, *Modern World Movements*, where he wrote that he found no particle of difference between the aims and ideals of H.P. Blavatsky and those of accredited representatives of the Great School of Natural Science. He went on to say that after the founding of the Theosophical Society in 1875 'another *Great World Movement* loomed on the horizon, and having already gained great prominence, promised to absorb public attention.' After a lengthy correspondence with Florence Huntley, prior to 1903, Buck was able to establish that she derived none of her knowledge from the printed sources of Theosophy but was trained by a 'Master' of the School, thus indicating that her source and that of the 'School' was the same as Blavatsky's. TK, he wrote, often speaks of the Great School as the *University of the Universe* where 'all its methods, teaching and results, involve and unite the Physical and the Spiritual natures of man together.' Buck concurred with Richardson, that by obeying the Constructive Law of Nature in Individual Life, by exercising self-control and regarding 'Personal Responsibility', an individual could advance towards 'Mastership'.

This road to Mastership, as summarised by Buck and laid out in detail by Richardson in his *The Great Work*, was what appealed to Freeman.

He read the book numerous times and passed it on to friends and family in an effort to convert them to its teachings. *The Great Work* is divided into thirty-eight comparatively short chapters with titles such as Nature's Constructive Principle, Mastership, Morality, Spirituality and Self-Control. While it is beyond the scope of this book to go into great detail on Richardson's teachings, by drawing on a few examples it is possible to inquire why Freeman fell under the influence of TK and what motivated him to declare that 'the greatness of this *Great Work* looms steadily larger and larger in my mind. I mean to make my service to the School; the guiding principle of my life.'

Freeman, even before his acquaintance with TK's works, referred constantly to his desire to achieve Mastership; a goal that TK promised could only be attained by a committed and assiduous pupil. Ever since AJF's acquaintance with the writings of GBS, and from his first introduction to the 'occult world', he aimed to develop a 'higher power' in himself, as seen initially in the concept of Shaw's *Life Force*. The philosophy of *The Great Work* appears to be informed by similar concepts to those found in Shaw's *Man and superman* and other late nineteenth and early twentieth century philosophical works that responded to and challenged Darwin's theory of evolution, in particular the concept of natural selection. The 'Neo-Lamarckian' challenge to Darwinism posited that living things could to some degree develop characteristics during their lifetime, faculties that would then be inherited by their offspring, thereby allowing individuals greater control over their own destiny, as opposed to only advancing in the genetically deterministic Darwinian view.

Shaw's evolutionary ideas were based on his concept of the emerging *Life Force* joining human beings in a gradual physical, intellectual and moral transformation, resulting in greater powers of contemplation and self-realization that would in the long-term lead to perfection, or in Richardson's words, the realisation of 'Mastership'. An example of this thinking can be found in *The Great Work*:

> Through the intelligent exercise of our individual Powers we may
> place ourselves in perfect alignment with the Constructive Principle

of Nature in Individual Life, and thereby add to Nature's evolutionary impulse our own intelligent effort. The inevitable result of
this intelligent cooperation with Nature is the attainment of individual Mastership, in due course of time. Thus, we demonstrate the
interesting fact that while Nature, of her own accord and by her
unaided effort, evolves a Man, it requires the added impulse of
man's own individual intelligent effort, acting in harmony with
Nature, to evolve a Master.

Richardson also criticised modern science and its methods when he wrote
that scientists would never discover the reality of another world beyond
the physical as they were limited to 'only one process, or one method',
whereas in order to prove the reality of life after death, a scientist would
need to develop 'within himself... Spiritual perception.' While Richardson
wrote at length about the ability of the individual to develop and exercise
his spiritual senses and turn from the physical to the spiritual plane of
existence, neither he nor other writers such as Huntley, gave much
concrete detail on how to achieve this. Instead, these writers tended to give
advice on developing personal, moral qualities and self-control, which
were ideas Freeman had encountered before in works like Lubbock's *Use
of Life* and other popular self-help manuals of the day. Thus, the practical-
ities of achieving Mastership remained elusive.

One concrete suggestion for how to attain Mastership was to develop
Temperance, because, as Richardson put it, 'no man who fails to exercise
self-control over the indulgence of his appetites, passion, emotions and
desires within constructive limits need ever expect or hope to achieve
Spiritual Mastership... Temperance is the remedy for all human excesses.'
Self-control, Knowledge, Possession, Soul and Diet were other themes
briefly discussed in the book and it is rather surprising that Richardson
suggested that the eating of a purely vegetarian diet was not necessarily
conducive to spiritual or moral development seeing it as a religious 'dogma'.
How Freeman reacted to this we do not know, but he still refused to eat meat.

Freeman had long sought a spiritual philosophy that reconciled
science with occultism, and although there was much to find fault with in

Richardson's work, Freeman instead found food for his soul in the Guru's writings. However, one may question why the abundant range of Theosophical publications didn't give AJF the same satisfaction, or why Christian Science, of which he was an avid reader and a participant at their meetings, didn't appeal to him as strongly. Perhaps what drew the young Arnold Freeman so powerfully to *The Great Work* was its promise of a 'scientific' challenge to Darwin's theory of evolution, written with reference to spiritual development.

Similarly it was evolutionary concepts which Freeman relished in Huntley's book *The Harmonics of Evolution*, noting after he had finished it that he had found some answers to his questions about sex and marriage:

> To this problem I have received in one sense an answer from TK's other book *The Harmonics of Evolution*. This is as wonderful in its own way as *The Great Work* and dazzles me by the light it throws on the whole meaning and purpose of sex. The fundamental proposition of the work is that the individual finds perfect happiness only in a perfect marriage, and Providence has arranged for each perfected man a perfected woman to complete him or her... this quite changes my perspective. I have never despised love, but I have never ultimately thought of it in this way.

Through reading this book Freeman resolved the conflict he experienced between the red passions of sex and the white passion of love as found in H. G. Wells's novel *The New Machiavelli*. In his past relationships, he recalled, 'if I have resolved to suppress the red passions it is only in order that the white may have free play. But the red will not be suppressed! And here is my future master saying: Your duty is to cultivate the red as well as the white... a perfect harmonic.'

Sean Williams, a Master for an Eager Student

Freeman noted in his diary that Sean Williams appeared at a crucial time in his life. He had been searching for some time for a spiritual path that could lead him towards 'Mastership' and it was Williams who, for approximately five years, acted as his mentor, guide, spiritual counsellor, advisor and friend on this journey. Williams was approximately thirty-five years older than Freeman, but despite this they met regularly, and shared numerous things in common including a love of Shakespeare and a fascination for the occult. Freeman adored Sean Williams, as he said in early 1911, he felt he'd 'struck diamond rather than gold' in finding him. 'He is the most cultured, the most erudite, the most gifted, the most spiritual and the most loveable of all my friends.' With reference to his profession as a dentist, Freeman decided that this made him a 'leader in his own scientific world… he talks beautifully; his erudition is extensive and his character truly finished… he is going to introduce me to a little group of advanced students in occultism that he believes will be forming in a few weeks… when the pupil is ready the Master appears! So far my life has been a search for the Path… there is far to go before Master-ship… but I am on the path and the goal is sure.' It seems that AJF really believed that an 'Unseen Hand' had led him to meet Williams and that now he cared nothing for marriage or money, only the development of his character.

Williams was an American citizen, so any record of his biographical details in the UK is sparse. I have been unable to find his place and date of birth or anything about where he grew up or his educational background. However, there are copious biographical references to the man in Freeman's diaries. On the last few pages of the 1910/1911 diary, six months after Freeman had first met Williams, he describes an occasion one afternoon, when Williams had failed to turn up for an appointment at his house in George Street, Williams' secretary, Miss Usherwood, had told Freeman 'Some fresh revelation of his versatility and genius'. Apparently, Williams wrote poetry and had written a book on Sicily (published at seven pounds seven shillings), and one book on Shakespeare. Freeman went on to say that 'he is thought by many people to be the greatest dentist in practice… many of his patients wait months for him if he is away. In America they made a frightful fuss over him'. He notes further that Williams was very '*unbusinesslike*' in his habits and would get absorbed in one thing after another to the exclusion of all things else: photography, artificial teeth, painting, music, literature, travel, sculpture, his garden and religion. It appears that due to his lack of focus and scant knowledge of business skills Williams 'lost all the money he had accumulated by thirty years of dental work in unfortunate ventures, but he has made a great discovery... in methods of making artificial teeth... which if successful should bring in a handsome profit.'

It was after Williams' wife died in 1908 that he began to write poetry and a friend set one of his long poems, 'Love and Death', to music. He remarried, with two children from his first wife, 'one of whom married Herkomer's son' (Sir Hubert von Herkomer 1849-1914), while the other became a dentist with a practice in New York. His second wife, also previously married, was a close relative of John Greenleaf Whittier (1807-1892), an American Quaker poet and an advocate of the abolition of slavery in the United States.

Aided by his friend Sean Williams, Freeman studied TK's writings for the next six years. AJF hoped to use Williams to help persuade his family that the right thing for him to do was to travel to Chicago to study under TK as a personal student. He asked Williams to send TK his article from the Lancet as a way of introduction and proof of his ability to study and write, which Williams eventually did. During this time, Freeman was utterly captivated by *The Great Work*, describing how it 'arrested my attention more than any other I have read... *The Great Work* which I have just perused for the second time, is sufficient in itself to make me willing, nay eager, to follow the guidance of its author along the road to Master-ship.' During Freeman's time as an election campaigner for Hay Morgan in the 1910 election, he copied many extracts from *The Great Work* into his book of quotations, which are full of references to self-control, the conquering of fear, vanity and self-indulgence. 'I remember making out a list of the qualities that are the *Mark of the Master*, which I carried in my Macintosh pocket on the road to Cornwall and continually read and meditated upon them as I walked across Devon.'

Reading TK's work inspired Freeman so much that he sent copies to various prominent people, including Sir Oliver Lodge, because Sean Williams had assured him that Lodge had seen TK's books. However, he eventually received a letter from Sir Oliver Lodge's secretary telling him that 'Sir Oliver has no recollection of reading any of TK's books and has no knowledge of him… he cannot give personal interviews to strangers unless there is a special reason.'

By December 1910 and into January 1911, Freeman was already anticipating how his spiritual development, working under the guidance of TK, would unfold. On New Year's Eve 1910 he wrote:

> For my spiritual development I hope to be under TK's guidance… I know how imperfect my character is. My self-control is most limited and a slight extra pressure from outside always causes a leakage of anger or lust or self-indulgence. I want to be God-like, calm and restrained… it is that spirit of complete renunciation that will save the world. But the great work is to love. I have always been true to that earlier vision of mine, to live for others… the joy of helping others, as I shall one day be able to do will be a reward a thousand times worth all the privation that the struggle demands.

In the first few months of 1911 Freeman met Williams on a number of occasions, sometimes for dinner at his home in Fellows Road, Hampstead or at Eustace Miles's vegetarian restaurant. In a short time, he began to trust Williams's advice implicitly, based on the impression he made and his comprehensive scientific, occult and cultural knowledge. He found Williams to be a 'tip-top man in his profession… he looks after the teeth of any number of titled people, including Annie Besant and Alcyone, and appears to know all the celebrities… he said he hoped that I should be one of those who would take a prominent part in the Movement that the Christ would set afoot when he comes.' In early January 1911 Williams agreed to write a letter of introduction to TK, with Freeman adding an introductory letter of his own.

On Tuesday February 7th, 1911, Freeman received a letter from TK which he found to be courteous and sympathetic while informing him that it was practically impossible for him to be taken on as a personal pupil. 'Instruction', TK wrote, 'is very time consuming for both instructor and pupil and the most vital parts cannot be given by correspondence'. He therefore suggested a preliminary course of study over two years.

Freeman was not too happy about this and consulted Sean Williams to explore alternatives. He remained, however, 'strongly attached' to the idea of going to Chicago and offering to work for TK for free. Freeman had some money saved up and hoped to negotiate with his brother Peter to free up his share in the family business which he would not normally have received until the death of his mother. AJF lived mainly on money given to him by his mother, so he knew that he faced objections from his family if he wanted to pursue his path; they were already complaining about Freeman 'not earning a living… they will think me insane.'

However, Freeman also knew that because of his commitment to his work with the Webbs and his DSc studies, he would have to wait at least a year before deciding to go to the USA. He discussed these problems with Williams, who convinced him that studying under TK would be of immense benefit in the future. One evening after dinner Williams told him that:

> If you go out to TK determined to come back to England and do a greater work than any of the present leaders of English Thought are doing, you can do it. There's no doubt about it… you can do greater work in this country than had ever been done before or than anyone is doing here.

Such 'wise counsel', about which Freeman was understandably enthusiastic, led him to believe that his destiny lay in revitalising 'the springs of thought in this country, influencing men like Shaw, Webb and Wells as I assuredly can if I become a Master and so by teaching the teachers, teach the world… after my training under TK I shall have a religion. I shall know of a certainty that God and Free Will and the Future Life are unquestionable certainties… my work will be to make England religious just as Webb has made it socialistic.' Convinced, and even blinded by this gross overestimation of his and TK's abilities, Freeman began to make serious financial and strategic plans to go to Chicago.

It was also Williams' influence that caused Freeman to question the value of finishing his DSc thesis. 'I must confess that every time I ask the question, I answer it affirmatively with less assurance.' So, he began to formulate arguments against completing his thesis. Originally, he thought it would make an important contribution towards making changes in social legislation, but now he doubted whether that was even possible. Even though he had been studying history and economics at Oxford, 'my heart has been in philosophy and spiritual things.' At that time, he thought he could help humanity through economics but now he was increasingly convinced of a better way, and despite his family thinking 'he is mellowing and respectable, I fear that means degeneration and stagnation.'

After completing his degree his family expected him to take up a lectureship in economics, but Freeman was less confident in that future, asking 'what on earth am I supposed to say? Imagine me trying to explain occult development to Don or Hay Morgan. Mother may understand, but mother is always so prudent and unadventurous that she will ultimately be hostile to this enterprise.' AJF believed that the members of the family who would support him were Peter and Daisy whilst all the others would think him:

> Actually insane… and in all this I have scarcely once considered, the fundamental question of why I am going. I suppose it is because I cannot help it. Every other door is locked, barred and bolted. All my yearnings and efforts since boyhood have brought me to this door and now I cannot but knock for it to open. *The Great Work* tells me something of what I shall find when I have passed through. I know that it will be knowledge such as I prize beyond all other and I know that in gaining it, I am doing my best for the world.

The Anguish of the Threshold

All the while, Arnold's thesis work was largely abandoned, having only finished the part on 'Special Assessments on Relations under the Poor Law Authority', as he contemplated 'all the deep and tender relationships that I will be forced to tear up by the roots and leaving half-finished that work on which I have spent two years!' He planned to finish the thesis chapter in three weeks and then go and visit Peter in Penarth to 'talk over the whole matter', with a fierce determination and firm resolution to go to Chicago in September. Freeman was in an inner turmoil and agonised over the decisions he needed to confront:

> Surely the Final Resolve is forming itself in the subconscious mind and that will be my guide in the end. There are many conflicting feelings at present. The bounding joy that I felt at first has given way to doubt and anxiety, but every now and then the pure thought of being a Master and perhaps of making the perfect marriage comes to lift me from sorrowfulness. I am not down hearted but I see fighting ahead and then beyond that – the Unknown!

Finally, he decided to introduce Sean Williams to his mother and brother Ralph who reluctantly agreed that he should go to Chicago and talk to TK about what he should do. Freeman had, however, made up his mind months ago and didn't need anyone's permission to go out there, writing, 'I shall simply go out to Chicago and stay there. TK can't decide what I ought to do, it isn't even right to ask him. I am the only person who can give a decision.'

The one issue that caused Freeman to hesitate was whether it was his 'duty' to finish the DSc. He found this prospect, 'a distinctly distasteful task, especially as I feel that my heart will not be in the research… I can't avoid the feeling that if I do that it will be in the spirit of false martyrdom.'

On September 18th, 1911, he finally received a letter from Sean Williams that TK had written to him:

> My dear Arnold, I arrived home last night and found a long letter from TK. It is a remarkable letter and while there is much that is encouraging in it, you will be greatly disappointed in finding that it puts a decided negative on your proposal to go to Chicago. Come to George Street tomorrow (Monday) if you can at about noon and we will lunch together and talk matters over.

Freeman transcribed the letter from TK into his diary and, as Williams indicates, it was a 'remarkable letter.' Remarkable first for its length (it covers 19 pages of A5), and secondly for TK's gentle and persuasive, yet strident opposition to Freeman travelling to Chicago. In a cogent argument he carefully outlined the reasons why it was neither practical nor possible for him to offer Freeman any type of work in the Great School. Freeman, TK wrote:

> Has taken a good many things for granted, without realising the possibility that there is absolutely nothing he could do at present that would be of the slightest service to me in the accomplishment of the tasks before me… this work from beginning to end is strictly confidential work of such nature that none can be admitted to its responsibilities, save those who have been regularly prepared for that specific purpose.

TK went on to say that even if Freeman did present himself at the door of the School it was incumbent on every student who wanted to gain admittance to 'first prove his knowledge and understanding of the teachings by passing a thorough, searching, exhaustive and exacting examination covering the entire subject matter of the three "test" works of the Harmonic Series.' In addition, each student was 'compelled to prove not only his knowledge of the teachings… but also that he accepts them unequivocally.' TK then suggested that Freeman stay at home and prepare himself for examination by correspondence course, and then continue for another two or three years and progress through the School until he achieved admission to the Ethical Section.

Surprisingly Freeman was 'overjoyed' with the news as he could now remain at home with friends and family, learn French and German, continue with his education, and 'pick up music and other interests' he wished to develop. He decided, however, not to continue with his DSc and to 'lay it aside conscientiously.' In the ensuing conversation with Williams, they discussed how they could find some means of spreading TK's ideas in England, and it is evident that Williams was becoming more and more involved in Freeman's life and had gained greater influence over his decision making. 'He is the one among all my friends who I do not "exhaust". I mean I have still much to learn from him.'

Gaston De Mengel

Another interesting connection in Freeman's 'occult world' was with the British occultist Gaston De Mengel, who was later a member of the Alchemical Society and published articles in their journal. De Mengel is known later in his life to have had connections to the French secret society the Brotherhood of Polaries. Himmler also recruited him to instruct the Nazis on the links between pre-Christian Indian, Persian and Chinese literature and the Edda, Vedas, and Kabbalah. De Mengel's works on Agartha and Shambhala were translated into German where they were used to prove the existence of an 'Atlantean-Aryan' world triangle or geomantic 'axis', that connected the Nordic countries with France, South Asia and Tibet.

We know from the diaries that Freeman belonged to a secret brotherhood in London, and it was De Mengel who provided him with 'the earlier sheets of a course of initiation into the Universal Brotherhood.' They met regularly at the De Mengels' house where they swore a 'solemn obligation of secrecy as regards proceedings… we are supposed not to let the outside world know that the Universal Brotherhood (UB) exists even! It is a secret society and has no direct or public contact with the world.' Freeman met eight other members including the De Mengels but the others he knew only by numbers as no names were revealed. In October, De Mengel informed him that anyone who had not reached a certain stage in the UB would not be allowed to attend any more meetings at his house, but Freeman was not perturbed by this as he wished to remain loyal to TK, although he was convinced that TK and the Great School were from the same source as the UB. He notes the following:

> TK was a guru of the same Brotherhood to which he has introduced me. I feel that TK's Great School and De Mengel's Universal Brotherhood and the Theosophical Brotherhood must all be one and the same. De Mengel has had the same struggle for freedom that I have and I rate his opinion highly… he advises me to go on with the training the Brotherhood is offering me through his agency and says that me going out to TK later will not in the least interfere with this.

At a later meeting in South Kensington De Mengel offered Freeman to 'form a "Matrix" for those who are in "dead earnest" to turn the knowledge given them by the documents of the Universal Brotherhood to practical account and I have agreed to do so.' AJF also discussed TK with De Mengel who appears to have changed his mind about TK, saying that he was not as great a teacher as Freeman thought he was, and that TK's school was not the Universal Brotherhood. Freeman respected and valued De Mengel's opinions for he regarded him as more experienced in 'these matters.'

Nothing more is mentioned in the diaries about De Mengel or the 'Secret Brotherhood', but Freeman's involvement in occult matters continued for the remainder of his life and his relationship with Richardson lasted until 1916. From 1909 onwards, however, AJF felt the need to at least begin some form of working life even if he didn't earn money by doing it. We know that he received an allowance from his mother and at a later date he was to receive something from his Father's inheritance, so unlike many others, there was no urgency for him to 'earn a living', but despite this, and possibly under pressure from his brothers, he decided to begin working with Sidney and Beatrice Webb.

Chapter Seven
A Working Life[28]

Sidney and Beatrice Webb

In the autumn of 1909 AJF began to work for the Webbs on their intensive program of publicity for the Minority Report, written by Beatrice Webb with the assistance of her husband Sidney. It was also around this time that Freeman was considering starting a doctorate at the LSE under the supervision of the Webbs on an as yet undetermined subject. His first joint meeting with them was on September 30th when he met them at their house, arriving early to discuss his DSc thesis. During the discussion the Webbs told him they were very pleased with the progress of the Committee for the Break Up of the Poor Law, which people were joining at the rate of one thousand per week. The DSc, Webb told him, should address something to do with the Minority Report, such as Charge and Recovery in Poor Relief, but Freeman remained unconvinced that this was the right subject for him. Throughout the final months of 1909 he consulted many leading scholars on the subject of what he should research; these included Hastings Lee-Smith, Chairman of the Executive Committee at Ruskin College, and later an expert on economics and Graham Wallas a coworker of the Webbs, one of the founders of the LSE and an expert on social psychology.

Beatrice Webb was appointed as a member of the Royal Commission on the Poor Law from 1905 to 1909, and, failing to turn the Commission to her way of thinking, produced a comprehensive policy on pauperism in the form of a Minority Report, which advocated universal social insurance and outlined a fledgling welfare state. This report was published in 1909 and the Webbs launched a national campaign for the Break Up of the Poor Law, publishing *The Prevention of Destitution* in 1911.

The Commission on the Poor Laws and Relief of Distress produced the Majority Report that largely supported the use of the Poor Laws to manage poor relief and recommended that it should be renamed 'public assistance'. The report reflected the feelings of some of the commissioners that poverty was the result of immorality and that the Boards of Guardians were providing too much outdoor relief to people. In contrast, the Minority Report, signed by four commissioners, including Beatrice Webb, argued for the abolition of the Poor Laws and the transfer of those functions to other institutions that could provide care. Her report focused on prevention rather than providing relief and it challenged the dominant assumption that the poor were solely to blame for their own poverty, demonstrating that the causes of poverty are structural as well as individual, and argued that society has a collective responsibility to prevent poverty, not merely alleviate it. It has been argued by some scholars that the Minority Report to the Poor Law Commission first set out the vision, arguments and values of social justice that were to become the foundations of the modern welfare state that first came into being after World War Two. It was, therefore, the Minority Report that AJF vigorously promoted, by travelling to various organisations both in and outside London; giving lectures and holding seminars. He was also an active participant and organizer of the National Conference for the Prevention of Destitution which took place in London in June 2011. Although he was very likely aware of the work that the Webbs were involved in, it was at a lecture in Oxford Town Hall on May 22nd 1909 that Freeman first heard Sidney Webb speak on the Poor Law Commission. Freeman was enthused about this 'wonderful piece of work... to get the proposals put into effect will mean to decrease the misery in England by one half in twelve or fifteen years.' He thought that 'if these proposals would be put into effect, it would produce a well-fed, healthy and educated people who will want Socialism.' In late July he was also active in sending all his friends the necessary forms to persuade them to join the National Committee for the Break Up of the Poor Law.

Freeman's work with Sidney and Beatrice Webb was broadly a part-time voluntary post as he also did some occasional research work for the Board of Trade at just over £4 a week, all expenses paid, six hours a day; investigating the conditions of juvenile employment in the building trade. This work occupied him for a time, and he recalls in the diaries finding it 'very satisfying interviewing builders, electricians and leather workers in order to find openings for boys when they leave school.' This work was similar to the research he undertook later at Woodbrooke and probably gave him the skills needed to complete the project as successfully as he did.

It is apparent from the diaries, and the regular meetings Freeman held with the Webbs, that they built up a close working relationship. On one visit to Beatrice Webb about 'the Break Up of the Poor Law propaganda', he had a very long meeting with her and another associate. He describes her as:

> Charming with a nose like a hawk, betokening her masculine qualities… I asked her definitely before I went if she was quite certain that we were working towards a civilisation at last.

Beatrice replied that England would be a much more beautiful place fifty years from now, and this, Freeman remarks, from someone who had as much opportunity of knowing as anyone. He also asked for her advice on the work he was doing at the LSE, because he was thinking of doing the BSc rather than a doctorate. Beatrice advised him against this and recommended again that he complete a DSc on 'Charge and Recovery' in connection with the Minority Report. In this context the main proposals of the Report were, in contrast to the Majority Report, more specifically aligned to meeting the needs of the destitute. The conscious purpose of the Minority Commissioners was to confine their proposed Public Assistance to those whose private means were insufficient to meet the then current Standard of Efficiency. What the Report suggested was the elimination of the choice by Local Authorities whether or not to treat a person, which officials based on their often-unfounded assumptions about the ability of those in need to pay for their own treatment. So, Beatrice agreed with her husband that this would be a fruitful line of enquiry for Arnold. He eventually started working on a DSc on Monday 18th October, which he noted 'will occupy most of my time and Yogi development will occupy much of the remainder.' Arnold doesn't mention here that a substantial amount of his work with the Webbs involved giving talks and lectures, mainly in and around the London area, on the Minority Report and the Break Up of the Poor Law. It appears that this too occupied much of his time, as he travelled to St Albans, Luton, Bedford and Stoke on Trent and gave lectures on unemployment at the Adult School and lectured at the Young Men's Society and various other institutions.

It was in the spring term of 1910 that AJF acted as an assistant lecturer at the London School of Economics, helping Sidney run the seminar known as Seasonal Trades. The seminar was aimed at students who were new to research, and sought to 'enable those who take part to discover for themselves how to study a given subject... to accustom the students to use different methods of investigation and the principal sources of information and make them realise by personal experiment and mutual criticism both how such studies are apt to fall short of accuracy and completeness, and in what manner these defects may be remedied.' In the preface to the published volume on these seminars, Sidney Webb wrote that it was 'his assistant Mr Arnold Freeman' who was responsible for putting the book together.

Freeman also played a major role in organising The National Conference for the Prevention of Destitution, which was held at Caxton Hall, Westminster from May 30th to June 2nd 1911. Hundreds of prominent personalities from the world of politics, culture and high society, as well as from various agencies of a non-party and non-sectional character from all over the United Kingdom, met to discuss how best to promote the findings of the Minority Report. In the preface to the published proceedings it states that nothing of the kind had previously been organized as a common meeting ground for all those concerned with the problem of preventing, as opposed to merely relieving, destitution. The conference lasted three-and-a-half days, and was crammed full with over three hundred papers and over one hundred speeches. The only way to organize this great productivity was to divide the conference into different sections, which included, among others, the Legal and Financial Section of which AJF was Honorary Secretary together with his colleague Herman Henry Schloesser (1883-1979) (later Slesser), a young barrister who became Solicitor General under the Labour Government in 1924 and was Knighted in the same year. Freeman submitted a paper on the 'Basis of Ability to Pay', a term dating back to the 1601 Elizabethan Act which empowered parish overseers to raise money for poor relief from the inhabitants of the parish, according to their ability to pay. Failure to pay the poor-rate used to result in a summons to appear before a Justice of the Peace who could impose a fine or the seizure of property, or even prison.

It is difficult to ascertain from the diaries exactly when AJF's work for the Webbs came to an end. In the Autumn of 1911, the Webbs left England for a long-planned world tour; visiting Japan, China and Canada, to name a few of their destinations. Looking back on this time Beatrice was convinced that the Minority Report on the Poor Law and the Anti-destitution campaign had been a great success. As she notes in her diary on June 3rd, 1911, 'the Conference was a great success... when we come back next spring we shall have to decide what is to be done – whether we are to close up, or to go on or to divide the work between the National Conference and the Fabian Society.' Earlier she noted that because of the success of the conference, she felt an obligation to convert 'England... to the prevention of destitution' and it was time for a genuine Socialist party in Britain with a viable programme for reform and a workable philosophy.

After their world tour, however, Beatrice thought that their old ideas were out-dated and their efforts for eradicating poverty were effectively wiped out while they were away. In this context it is noteworthy that Sidney said to AJF in February, after their joint seminar on 'Seasonal Unemployment in the Building Trade', that the responsibility for continuing with the work lay with him while the Webbs were away. For his part, Freeman felt 'rather a hypocrite', because of his plans to go to Chicago. So, on the evidence from the diaries, Freeman's work with the Webbs effectively ended when they left England in the early summer of 1911, although he did remain in contact with them on a more personal level.[29]

A Trip to Germany

Freeman's stated motivation to travel to Germany in June 1911 was to take a holiday, but from the diary entries it appears to have been more of a philosophical quest, as he visited both Ernst Haeckel and Rudolf Steiner. The trip was carefully planned, with a travel timetable and accommodation arranged long in advance.

After crossing on the mail and passenger steamer from Queenborough to Flushing, and then taking trains to Hannover, he eventually found his host family consisting of Otto Kustermann and his wife, son and daughter at Königsworther Str. 47. It was here on July 1st that Freeman wrote to his mother, telling her of his plans to go to Chicago in September: 'In this month comes the explosion! I feel like an Anarchist, secreting a bomb and waiting for the right moment to throw it. My letter will certainly drop like a bomb among my friends; too much of a bomb I fear.'

He is mostly impressed by the city of Hannover and one thing he did learn, after observing the German people and their customs, was 'to understand the English Royal Family'.

> I can quite comprehend why George II didn't like bunting or poetry. I can see why George III was such a pig-headed fool, why Victoria was so beloved of the stupid, mediocre, stodgy English and I can shrewdly suspect that the deadly virtues of the earlier Georges are reproduced in our present monarch.

Freeman travelled from Hannover to Hildesheim and then on to Hamelin, where on the train he had a flirtatious encounter with a 'fair damsel'. This 'damsel' was Maria Hoos of Poststrasse 19, Lehrte, who interrupted her journey to show him round the town. Freeman asked her an assortment of questions, including whether she was a vegetarian (she wasn't) and whether she knew Steiner (she didn't).

On Thursday 6th July, he left Hannover for Berlin and arrived at 17 Motzstrasse to find that Peter's theosophical friend Ilsie Mackenzie was away. The caretaker then found Fraulein Lehmann who sought and found a friend who spoke English, so Freeman was eventually given a room on the floor where Rudolf Steiner normally resided. He spent his first day exploring parts of the city and on the second day Fraulein Lehmann and Herr Reebstein took him for a meal and stroll in the Zoological Gardens. On Sunday and Monday he continued exploring the city and writing letters, and on Tuesday 11th he travelled to Jena to see Ernst Haeckel.

> After a pleasant rest in the sun… I made my way to Ernst Haeckel's Strasse and found Haeckel's house after one or two enquiries… in a few minutes I was on the balcony sitting down by the Professor. He was half lying and half sitting in a dark chair with a scientific book half open on a table at his side… he was one of the jolliest men I have ever met… he laughed all the time, about himself, about the world, about religion, about death, about God, about science.

Haeckel explained that he had had a fall 12 weeks prior and broken his thighbone. Freeman relates that from the very beginning of their conversation Haeckel assumed he was a 'Materialistic Monist', and he did not trouble to correct him or state his own views… so I let him talk on and just asked questions. Freeman told him he 'knew Steiner' and was going to visit him. Haeckel responded by telling him to give his kind regards and to say that he was 'glad to hear he had ascended into heaven and later when I was going told me to tell Steiner that he (Haeckel) was a lost soul'. Haeckel explained to the other Professor that Steiner was a very queer case of a man who had once been a materialistic monist and was now a 'spiritualist', theosophist etc. The reason for this, Haeckel claimed, was that Steiner had not studied natural science. Haeckel told Freeman that for a long time he was religious due to his training… he said that the battle between Materialism and Mysticism was as old as Ancient Greece and referred to the wealth of opinions then. They talked of other things such as immortality and thought transference, which Haeckel believed was possible, but still could be explained in scientific terms. Just before he left AJF told Haeckel he intended to read his Evolution of Man and Haeckel answered by saying, 'Oh well, I have not worked in vain.'

The next day, Wednesday 12th, Freeman travelled on the overnight train to Munich to visit Rudolf Steiner. He tells the following story:

It was not altogether a satisfactory interview, for I had nothing in particular to see him about and he was halfway through tea when I arrived. I told him I wanted to speak to him about my life and we agreed to meet at Karlsruhe in October. I gave him a part of Haeckel's message and we agreed that Haeckel was hopelessly materialistic. We really talked about nothing worth relating; we were discussing whether I could see him next day and why I must go etc. But I met him and that was all I wanted. He is a fine man. I liked his complete abandon. He did not look as though he had shaved for a week and his collar was unkempt and dirty. He wore a shabby frock-coat and in the total ensemble looked exactly like a low comedian. He might have passed for that in the street to those who do not read face, but his face is that of a great man. He has a wonderfully kind smile; you can see that he is a great thinker and there is something deep and wonderful about him that I did not find in Haeckel… [who] represents the 19th century; he typifies the older science; he is the last of the materialists. Steiner stands for the 20th century and the coming science. I suppose that Haeckel and Steiner are the two greatest thinkers in Germany today and I have interviewed them both within four and twenty hours!

After his visit he ate in a vegetarian restaurant, explored Munich and with a rare prayer to God he posted the letter off to his mother. 'Oh! I do pray that she will enter into the spirit of my resolve and encourage me.' From Munich he travelled on to Venice via Trento where he spent a few hours and then continued for a very short visit to Belluno, before travelling to Cortina where he received a wire from Sean Williams informing him that 'important affairs prevented him from leaving,' which turned out to be Williams working on Annie Besant's teeth. 'He says her neglect of her mouth is almost incredible in a woman of such ideals.'

Funds were running low so Freeman sent home for more money and also received a letter from Julia Stuart Points suggesting that they could meet in Berlin on the 15th, but because of the distance he decided against it. He must have been feeling extraordinarily lonely as he writes:

I hope that the next time I travel here it will be with Mrs Arnold Freeman. Oh! How I long to take someone in my arms. Someone that is mine, mine, mine. I want to worship and be worshipped.

Money eventually arrived from home and he travelled continuously from Tuesday 18th to the morning of Thursday 19th when he arrived back in London to be invited by his mother into the garden for a conversation about his plans to go to Chicago:

During the morning mother and I had a talk in the garden; – the first word mentioned about my letter. Mother opened the conversation by asking me how long I had this project in my mind and then in a broken inconsequential way (for mother's mind easily switches from one train of thought to another), we discussed the various aspects of my plan. She was very kind and as sympathetic as I would expect. She said from the first that she would give me the money and more than that because I couldn't live on £65, but with the condition that I would finish my DSc work.

Freeman was, however, determined not to finish his Doctorate and was even more determined to get his own way and travel to Chicago. Mother told him that he needed to speak to Ralph and other members of the family who had read his letter and also read Richardson's *The Great Work*. That evening he went over to the Edmonsons' and Bert gave him his full support advising him 'to take no notice of what people say.' On the other hand his brother Ralph remained fairly non-committal and suggested he speak to Oliver Lodge, but did finally concede that if he felt it the right thing to do then he should go ahead. As we know from the previous chapter his plans to go to Chicago failed to materialise and his thoughts turned once more towards earning a living.

Woodbrooke and *Boy Life and Labour*

At the end of January 1912, Freeman wrote:

Perhaps in consequence of a diseased brain, brought about by ill health of late, I have begun to consider the possibility of earning an

honest living. I feel more and not less keenly the friction of being
at home.

So begins a determined search for regular paid employment, with
Freeman's thoughts leaning towards training to be a teacher, and by May
1912 he was hard at work on the Diploma in Education. He considered
teaching to be 'a noble profession… I shall learn the most valuable lessons
from the experience'. Simultaneously, he was applying for a number of
different academic posts, his priorities being to obtain a BLitt and to start
working seriously on his study with the Guru. In May 1912 he received a
letter inviting him for an interview for the research scholarship at
Woodbrooke Settlement. This triggered long term dreams, for he hoped
that this post would help him get his Diploma in Education, his diploma
in research at Birmingham, his BLitt at Oxford, an MSc (with geography)
at London and his eventual fellowship of the Royal Historical Society.
On the basis of these speculations, he travelled on Friday June 8th, 1912, to
Woodbrooke and was interviewed by John St George Heath (1885-1916),
a tutor in social studies and lecturer in Economics and later Warden at
Toynbee Hall.

The search for work continued successfully with a number of
opportunities opening up for Arnold. His first definitive offer, obtained
through a friend, was a teaching post from Manchester Grammar School.
Another idea came from Sidney Ball, who suggested a junior lectureship.
Ball was probably keen to have Freeman at Oxford as they both shared an
ardent commitment to social reform. He was well known in Oxford as a
passionate advocate of the systematic study of social problems, which
earned him the title of 'Oxford's socialist don'.

Jack Pease (1860-1943, later Lord Gainsford), who was at this time
president of the Board of Education, wrote to Freeman about the vacancy
of Vice-Principal at Ruskin College, which perhaps demonstrates the
extent of Freeman's political connections. Soon after, he was offered the
post but refused it! Virgo at the Joint Scholastic Agency 'begged' him to
take a position at the Strand School. He carefully considered his future
financial options and weighed up the possibilities of not doing

Richardson's work and finally decided that: 'these conclusions make me feel that even if I get an offer from Woodbrooke I shall refuse it.' One possible reason that he appears to be so indecisive about taking any of these posts is that financially he was reasonably secure due to the money he received from his father's legacy, and he had accrued some capital.

Freeman eventually applied for the post at the Strand School and on the same day received a letter from Woodbrooke offering him the research scholarship. He discussed it with his mother and 'felt inclined to take it'. Reflecting on his future finances he also revealed that he would receive £100-£150 per annum from his share in the family business. So, by the end of June, he had decided to take up the research at Woodbrooke and began to investigate a potential project.[30]

George Heath helped him in this search and suggested the project 'The Teaching of Civics' for a thesis, but insisted that Arnold give up his Diploma in Education so he could devote himself entirely to the research. Freeman sought advice on this at Oxford and after consultations at Oxford on a BLitt thesis with Ernest Barker (1874-1960, later Sir Ernest Barker) he was strongly advised that such a subject would not be appropriate, and Heath changed his mind and also advised AJF against it. The suggestion was that the project cover something in line with the educational proposals of the Minority Report, something which Freeman knew well because of his extensive knowledge of the Report. He wrote to Sidney Webb for advice and it was most likely under the influence of Webb that he eventually chose the topic of 'Boy Life and Labour'; a topic that was one of the priorities of the Royal Commission on the Poor Law. Webb had already advised him in June 1912 that if he went to Woodbrooke he should make sure 'that it results in something definite, because, you know, you drag your past about with you as it were.'

Freeman spent Michaelmas Day, 29th September 1912, at Woodbrooke with his sister Daisy, arranging his research work. Initially the focus of his project was on Boy and Girl Labour, but he finally settled on 'Boy Life and Labour'. By October he was well into the research, looking at the cards from the Labour Exchange, visiting Birmingham Schools and persuading the head teachers to get the boys to fill out his forms. He also went to the homes of his 'subjects', cross-questioning the parents and the boys. Freeman notes the following:

> Keeling of the Labour Exchanges called at Woodbrooke last Tuesday or Wednesday and we saw a great deal of each other. He is going to give me a mass of stuff for my investigation and thinks I might get a job as an investigator for the Labour Exchange.

AJF's research focused on the problem of the school leaving age and the perceived difficulties of boys entering 'dead-end jobs' with no training or education and becoming quite unemployable by the time they reached eighteen. Concern was also directed towards the moral effects of leaving school early. It was thought that young working-class boys and girls who enjoyed their leisure on the streets, in music halls and picture houses, were outside of adult control, and without a good schooling it was not possible for them to become 'good citizens'. Part of the research was also to find out why large numbers of boys became failures so early in life. As Freeman wrote in his introduction: 'the impressionable period of adolescence', between the ages of fourteen and eighteen, 'instead of being devoted to training as nature intended, is sacrificed to the immediate profit of industry'.

On New Year's Eve 1912, Freeman paused to reflect on the past year. He was not quite halfway through his research project at Woodbrooke and wrote that 'life lies plainer ahead of me now.' He believed that 'by this time next year I shall be earning a living with an income of about £200 a year; Nora will be engaged to me.' He vowed to continue with *The Great Work*, but desired to become 'more conventional and more like a finished gentleman, more like Henry Drummond and less like Bernard Shaw.' He predicted that he would still be a socialist, 'but a more cautious and less bloodthirsty one.' His relationship with Nora appears to have initiated a change in his character; not only with respect to his politics, but also to his attitude to love, and in 1913 they did finally get engaged.

Sir Michael Sadler, who was then Vice Chancellor of the University of Leeds and a leading educationalist, was asked by AJF to write the preface to his research paper. Sadler outlined Freeman's methodological approach as follows:

To ascertain the causes of the deterioration in character and in
earning capacity which has been observed in a great number of boys
who fail to pass at once into the higher grades of labour but escape
the special temptations of street trading and casual employment.
He determined to take a sample of such boys when they had reached
early manhood and, by close individual inquiry into their experience and circumstances, to ascertain, if possible, what causes had
led to their relative failure.

The sample Freeman took included seventy-one boys whose life at home
he examined by acquainting himself with what he thought were the main
influences in their lives: boys' clubs, picture palaces, music halls, football
matches and cheap literature. A picture was thereby produced of the
influence of both industrial and non-industrial institutions on the boys in
their adolescent years. He found that an absence of good parental
influence and continuing education nullified any positive influences from
early education. Therefore, the abrupt termination of education at the age
of fourteen and the neglect of family, community and society on the development of the boy, during the period of adolescence, had a far more
negative effect than had been too readily associated with the blind-alley
occupation. Freeman's special attention to this developmental period in a
boy's life was what made his study unique. As he said himself, clearly influenced by the Webbs' preventive approach to poverty:

> In this study, accordingly, special attention has been paid to aspects
> of the problem that have been altogether or partially neglected by
> previous inquiries. The question is considered from the standpoint
> of the boy, as well as from that of industry; and a careful analysis has
> been attempted of the boy's personality and of the educational and
> social influences that condition his growth, as well as of the indus-
> trial conditions amid which he does his work. Thus the problem we
> have to consider is not what happens at 19 to a fraction of boy
> workers, but what is occurring between 14 and 19 to the great
> majority of them.

Freeman also examined the limitations on a boy's adolescent development imposed by hereditary factors. In doing this he referred, uncritically, to the most up-to-date scholarship on the psychology of adolescence which was, at the turn of the nineteenth-to-twentieth century, written by scholars heavily influenced by Social Darwinism. For example, when he was attempting to make sense of why some of the boys in the study excelled at school whilst others had a poor record of performance, he drew quite openly on the works of Francis Galton (1822-1911) and Karl Pearson (1857-1936) who were both proponents of eugenics and scientific racism. Freeman says: 'What I wish to insist on here is that many elementary scholars are born into the world with limited powers of self advancement because of their hereditary handicap.' He then quotes Galton's work on *Hereditary Genius* where he argues that he is convinced that 'no man can achieve a very high reputation without being gifted with very high abilities'. For the material in his chapter on early adolescence, AJF also supported his findings by drawing on the work of Granville Stanley Hall (1844-1924) who was influenced by Darwin's theory of evolution and by Ernst Haeckel's theory of recapitulation. He believed that the process of recapitulation could be sped up through education and force children to reach modern standards of mental capabilities in a shorter length of time. Thus, Freeman argued 'that the child in the earlier period reproduces the characteristics of a very remote and long protracted stage of race development, while adolescence represents the subsequent march of humanity upward from savagery to civilisation'.

The recommendations or remedies AJF suggested for the 'evils' he identified had, he argued, 'become urgently necessary', but it was not possible to alter the 'general features of either the social or the industrial structure upon which society is at present based; it can only concern itself with such modifications as will ensure to the nation's youth preparation for the functions of adult life.'

One of the main recommendations was 'the statutory reduction of the hours of juvenile labor'. 'This is a fundamental remedy' Freeman noted, upon which all others depend. If hours are reduced then this would leave more time for the boys to undertake an education that would build up physique, intelligence and character. He gave the example of the company Cadbury Brothers, who made physical training and continued education compulsory for all their army of juvenile workers. The firm reported that 'the renewed energy resultant upon the attendance at these classes fully repays them for the time lost by the boys.'

Something that remained with Freeman from his work on this research, was the belief in the need for continued education and that the community must provide for this type of education. As we shall see later in his discussions with H.A.L. Fisher, a reciprocal arrangement between education providers and the community to improve the education of the working man and woman was seen as essential in improving the general living and working conditions in industrial towns and cities.

Surprisingly, another one of Freeman's recommendations was for the boys to have some form of military training. As he put it:

> Substantial objections may be raised to military training on ethical grounds, but it would seem to offer the most hopeful suggestions for the sort of physical development the youth needs at this period. And, on the other hand, if it is the wish of the nation that we should establish a citizen army, this surely is the period when every boy might be given sufficient training to bring him up to the standards of the Territorial Force. Swimming, wrestling, boxing, running, jumping, gymnastics, perhaps even dancing, ought to form part of the boy's normal education.

Gardening and sufficient instruction in relation to sexual matters was also suggested, as was instruction upon the responsibilities and duties of citizenship. It appears that there was a growing awareness in Freeman's mind at this time of the importance of education in solving some of the social problems he encountered whilst conducting this project, and he quotes Tolstoy who said that 'you need three things – schools, schools and schools' to civilize a nation, and 'until we have learnt that lesson, and are prepared to give education as freely to the poor as to the rich, we shall continue the manufacture of inefficient workers and citizens. Nothing less than has been here suggested will suffice to rescue the oncoming genera-tion from the evil influences that beset the youth of today.'

Freeman's thinking, approach and conclusions reflect the social philosophy of the Webbs who conceived a social ethics that was embedded in their view of the reciprocal relationship between the individual and the community. They thought that character, personality and morals were socially determined and improvement in the moral tenor of society depended on a collective effort. Society had to be reorganized such that it was the obligation of the community to provide the necessary basis for human progress for all its citizens.

Freeman's research was eventually published as a book in 1914 and received some very favourable reviews, not only in this country but also in the USA. As one American reviewer wrote:

> Usually this class of book is apt to be loaded with laboured detail which may fascinate the few close students of the subject; but drive the general reader, who needs interesting, away in despair. Mr Freeman has avoided that mistake, and has given us a book that is deeply interesting in every page. It is a human study of a national problem. The conclusions he comes to may not be perfect, but if they could be adopted they would go far to set boys on the road to efficiency and valuable social service.

In his usual 'propagandist' style Freeman promoted the book by giving lectures in the north of England but especially in the Sheffield area where he was living when it was published and Oxford University awarded him his 'coveted' BLitt. By the end of 1913 he was already working for the Workers' Educational Association (WEA) and the University Extension Movement, and looking back over his work the previous year, Freeman reflected in his diary how for the first time in many years his life felt settled and 'free from worry.' His transition into the working world had brought him peace and purpose.

Chapter Eight

The Great War, Writing and Reconstruction

Workers' Educational Association

Never before in the history of Diarrhoea (not a bad name for the disease of diary writing), did a diarist forget his task for so long a period as I have done. (AJF, December 1913).

At this point in his 'diary writing life' AJF no longer felt the need to inscribe his innermost thoughts and feelings onto paper. Unlike, for example, the four diaries that cover the year 1911, the one '1914' diary that was written over a period of four years ending with some very short entries from 1917. Little mention is made of the First World War in the 1914-1917 diary, it contains mostly Freeman's inner struggle about his future: his aspirations to be an author, his work with Richardson (TK), his doubts about his ability to be a good lecturer and his relationship with his young family. Nevertheless, these years, as we shall see, were significant years for AJF; he found permanent work, got married, had his first child, severed his relationship with Richardson, and did much research, writing and publishing.

In April 1913 Freeman wrote that he 'came back hurriedly' from a break in the Isle of Wight for an opportunity to work for the Workers' Educational Association (WEA). He met Archibald Ramage, the Organising Secretary of the WEA, who was in London speaking at a Church of England Men's Society. On June 30th Ramage offered Freeman two classes in London and, in July, an offer of further work in Sheffield was made that was likely to lead to permanent employment. At the end of 1913, in his yearly review, Arnold recorded that 'the great thing about this year is that I have become settled. For the first time for many years, I have felt lately free from worry… my feet are firmly planted; I feel confidence in myself and know that I have a market value.' His sense of security strengthened when he was asked to take on an additional Economics class at Rectory Road for London University. He taught for eight weeks because the previous tutor was 'not popular with them, so I have gained esteem by his shortcomings.'

On July 11th, 1914, Nora White and Arnold James Freeman were married. The marriage took place in London where they were both living at the time and where Nora was teaching at the North London Collegiate School. His cousin Lawrence was best man as his brother Peter couldn't attend the wedding. They decided on Norway for their honeymoon. As was common at the time, Freeman arranged the whole trip by letter, writing to his friends in Norway, Lille and Kiss, and booking travel with Thomas Cook. His continued commitment to the teachings of TK reveals itself in his remark in the diaries that he and Nora were taking the Harmonic Series with them so that they could read and study it together. However, due to the outbreak of WWI, they had to cut short their honeymoon, and according to anecdotal evidence they stowed away on a Norwegian ship to get back to England by forging a close friendship with the captain. The couple moved to Sheffield immediately after the honeymoon, but not before Arnold went to the Board of Education to find out that he didn't get the job as a Junior Examiner. His comment on learning this news is revealing:

> Not getting that job at the Board of Education, where I would have rotted into a competent clerk, has set a seal, the Seal of Destiny, upon me.

The diaries from the early years contain some positive details about AJF's relationship with Nora and his family, while references to married life in later diaries are more about how Arnold sought to further his spiritual development to improve his relationship with Nora. An exception to this can be found in an entry from a few months into the marriage:

Nora is showing herself a splendid housewife. The thrills of the early married life have vanished... and we are settling down to a comfortable relationship, which will grow more pleasant if we grow more unselfish.

However, just before the birth of their first child Peter, in May 1915, the marriage came under strain because of Arnold's impulsiveness, so he resolved to try harder to make Nora more 'happy and self-possessed'. As Freeman put it, 'I am not kind enough. I get irritated and preach and speak in a hard tone and want my own way and find fault... I am up in arms in an instant if I don't get my own way.'

Nora and Arnold had three children. On the 5th May 1915 Peter was born, followed by their daughter Edith on 12th July 1919 and a second son, Christopher, on 11th September 1921. All three went on to lead successful lives. Peter started his career as a lecturer in Applied Science at the University of Sheffield and after moving to Cornwall became a translator of technical works from Russian and German. Edith, after graduating from Cambridge, lectured in history and was also secretary to the United Nations Association in Sheffield. She eventually moved to Suffolk and worked voluntarily for the Conservation Society. Christopher became Professor of Science Policy Studies at the University of Sussex. As we shall see later, Nora was very active in looking after refugee children during the Second World War, and was also an engaged supporter of the peace movement, so the Freeman home was invariably a busy and happy one. However, anecdotal evidence tells us that later in their marriage, the relationship between Arnold and Nora took a turn for the worse, but concrete details about this are not available.

Back in Sheffield, Freeman renewed his acquaintance with H. A. L. Fisher who at the time was Vice Chancellor of Sheffield University, and who had very likely taught him modern history at Oxford. Before the honeymoon, Fisher offered him work with the University Extension Movement, with the promise of more permanent work in the following years and a starting salary of £250 per year.[31] It was their mutual belief in the transformational power of education and their interest in promoting the 'Wisconsin Model of Education' at Sheffield that animated their conversations. The Wisconsin model contends that the beneficent influence of the university reaches out into the wider community enabling every citizen, irrespective of ethnic, social or economic background to benefit from the knowledge and discoveries created at the University, and, by extension, others in the nation and wider world. The university of Wisconsin's mission statement refers to the transmission of knowledge and values that would 'ensure the survival of this and future generations and improve the quality of life for all'. So Freeman and Fisher's joint interest was to bring a university education to people who would not normally have the opportunity to experience higher education, an aim that Freeman began to realise later at the Settlement.

Fisher was a formative influence on him at this stage and it was he who encouraged Freeman to participate and teach seminars at the university on economics and social studies. The seminars, given in the winter of 1913/1914, formed the basis of Freeman's 1914 booklet: *An Introduction to the Study of Social Problems*, published by the Workers' Educational Association with a preface by Fisher and a prefatory note by Albert Mansbridge, the General Secretary of the WEA. In his preface, Fisher outlined the virtues of a university education for the 'working man', for which the WEA was largely responsible, especially in Sheffield, and he questioned how this might be achieved:

> The experience of the WEA supplies some answers to this question. All over the country workers have been found to join classes where teaching of a University type is given… and to emerge after three years study, not only with the equipment of tested knowledge… but also with something of real academic spirit… an alert readiness to interrogate facts and to abide by the award of reason.

Mansbridge also emphasised the benefit of such an education and how it served the community. His words were in keeping with the WEA's expressed objectives:

> It is the object of [the WEA] to supply a platform on which those

engaged in manual labour may meet those engaged in the profession of teaching to discuss the problems of education, and more
particularly those problems which concern the workers. It has no
policy to push, except the policy of making the best education
available to all... Culture cannot be imposed upon any section of
the community from above: it must spring from the experience won
by men in their daily lives, and must reflect their own struggles,
aspirations and disappointments. (*The Highway*, October 1908).

Mansbridge also pointed out that the WEA was non-sectarian and didn't
owe loyalty to any political party. Neither gender, age nor social status
should make a difference to an individual's chances of attaining a university education that would enable them to transform their life. Equality was
a key principle for Mansbridge, as he illustrated in the case of a 74-year-
old woman 'who after powerful service to the community' went on to
eagerly study history, and philosophy of 'real university standard'. 'More
women', he continued, 'are coming into the movement in ever increasing
numbers. Many have been emphatic in declaring that thereby life has
become a new thing to them full of hitherto undreamed possibilities'.

        This view was endorsed on a more practical level by Freeman when
he reports that his classes were going extremely well as he had 'maintained
a full attendance and got nearly forty of the students and friends to attend
a social followed by a sort of Royal Commission on the relations between
the town and the university'. It was because of this and the possibilities he
saw for extending the activities of the university into the life of the town
that he had 'almost made up my mind to give myself up to Sheffield after
this season,' which, of course, he eventually did.

        Two other individuals must be mentioned at this juncture, both of
whom had some influence on Freeman at this point in his life. During
1913/1914, before his marriage to Nora, Arnold was still living in London
and commuting to Sheffield where he cultivated close friendships with
Lady Mabel Smith (1870-1951) and George H. McNeal (1874-1934).
Lady Mabel was a local socialist politician and later a board member
of the Sheffield Educational Settlement (SES), who shared Freeman's

commitment to socialism and adult education. She offered him 'hospitality every Thursday at Maltby. She and Major Smith are most pleasant people to meet, she is keenly interested in all this educational work'. They remained firm friends until her death in 1951. George McNeal was a friend of Nora's, and it is evident that the conversations Freeman had with McNeal played a part in the development of his ideas for future work in Sheffield. McNeal was a Wesleyan minister who made the following proclamation of intent when he opened Victoria Hall in 1908. It was to be a great evangelical preaching centre; the headquarters of a strong, vigorous and active Mission Church; a house of mercy in the centre of the city with an ever-open door; a people's home, the social and religious centre of their thought and activity; a rallying ground for all kinds of philanthropic and religious enterprise in the city. During their first meeting McNeal complained about how the university 'stands aloof from the town; he wants me to help bridge that chasm' and together they would do much towards making Sheffield a great university town.

World War One

Freeman hardly mentions the First World War in his diaries except for the occasional entry such as: 'No war news worth speaking of. Most of my friends either gone or just going to the front'. In 1914 he asked: 'ought I to fight?' However, he felt he could best serve his country by continuing his educational work rather than fighting in the trenches. He noted that military service was not yet compulsory, and that public opinion was against it. He was very unsure whether he wanted to fight and even wrote to Richardson in the USA to seek advice. His thirtieth birthday was approaching when the Government introduced conscription in March 1916, as voluntary enlistment could no longer meet the Armed Forces' need for recruits. Suddenly, all medically fit single men between the ages of 19 and 41 were deemed to have enlisted in the armed forces on 2nd March. In May 1916 a second Government act extended conscription to married men and the age limit was lowered to 18. Freeman probably claimed exemption from being 'called up' under the Scheduled Occupation classification of his profession as a teacher.

Despite the sparse references to the war, which seems at times conspicuous by its absence in his diaries, Freeman remained acutely aware of the political situation unfolding around him. He often conversed with Fisher who told him that the government was cutting down as much spending as they could, and Freeman was very angry when this affected his teaching after the cancellation of a class of his at Stoke Newington. This prompted a rant in the diaries about government policy, not only domestic, but also the strategies they were pursuing in Europe:

> God damn 'em!… I agree with Walt Whitman, things really look bleak just now. The Russians are being driven back like a flock of sheep and Fisher seemed to think when I saw him yesterday that the Germans would come back and do the same kind of thing in the West.

'Lloyd George's government', he goes on to say, 'is making a 'stampede for conscription', which, he believed 'will bring about a revolution in England as the workers are opposed to it – mainly because the Daily Mail has espoused it!' Surprisingly he makes the astute observation that whatever the outcome of the war there will be revolutions in both Germany and Russia. Sometime in the months between September and December 1915, Freeman declared that he would not serve, 'conscription or no conscription… No good ever really comes out of force and bloodshed… I would rather be shot as a traitor and coward'.

Freeman continued with his teaching but not without problems. During the summer of 1915 his class in London was observed by Alfred Zimmern (1879-1957), an inspector of the Board of Education, who had been involved since 1907 in working-class education. He had also been a fellow and tutor at Oxford from 1904 to 1909 so he probably knew Freeman there in his role as a history tutor. It was Zimmern's job to inspect adult education classes for their quality and effectiveness and warned Freeman against relying too much on his 'past accumulations of knowledge' and advised him to read 'big books'. Freeman castigated himself for this and thought that Zimmern felt his lecture was second rate. He admits that he had been concentrating too much on writing his novel and felt he ought to do better with his paid work, despite finding 'the temptation to write… irresistible.' One positive consequence of his fervour for writing was a book on essay writing technique, that he planned to develop with his relative Bernard Henderson for the WEA. It was published in 1915 with a preface by Mansbridge.

Becoming a Writer

In 1913 AJF's aspirations of carving out a literary career become more intense, with plans to produce propagandist stories embodying the ideas of The Great School and the Fabian Society and relating his own experiences of the spiritual plane of life. In June 1916 he felt inspired to visit the writer Arnold Bennett (1867-1931) to explore his deep reservations as to whether he would ever be a successful author. Apparently Bennett advised him to write for the market. 'My line of advance is that dictated by Arnold Bennett', he declared after the visit: 'Compromise! Write stories that will sell'. Bennett must have tried to persuade him away from writing the books that really interested him but to write for the commercial market, something that Bennett advocated in his book *The Truth About an Author* (1903), where the emphasis was on the commercial side of authorship. Freeman described this book as 'splendid… it has given me all the information I need to go on with my work and also encouraged me immensely'. He seemed to think that 'success depends not on genius, but on industry and perseverance'. This consolidated his conviction that his future lay in writing non-fiction, novels and stories; 'I can use my books for Socialism, Nature Care, The Great School, anything I care'. But despite his newly found security he still struggled to identify his true purpose in life. He frequently pondered the possibility of following George Bernard Shaw and developing his writing so as to become a political writer by contributing to different periodicals, propagating his views on socialism and religion, so that he could earn enough money to afford him the time for further study and agitation.

Freeman's most serious attempt at writing for a living began in October 1914 when he embarked on writing a novel called *The Furry Hand* and started negotiations with the publisher William Heinemann. Freeman was not new to writing imaginative stories; in the spring of 1906 he submitted a fairy story to the Skylark, his old school's magazine, which was published with the title of 'The Greatest Thing in the World'. In the autumn issue he had another story published called *The Masterpiece*, a morality tale based on the story of an artist who in the end dedicates his life to Jesus Christ. The 1907 spring issue contains another morality tale called 'Death and Life – A Parable', probably based on his reading of Charles Dickens, where the question is asked of the reader whether they are helping people to live or die: 'remember that every unkind word, every mean action… actually brings people nearer death. But every smile, every loving word, every unselfish action gives people life'. The autumn edition also contains a long historically themed poem called 'The Lovers' Leap' based on a chasm near Buxton. So his ambition to write imaginative fiction was hardly unfounded, but his meeting with Evans, a representative of Heinemann at the Authors' Club, in 1914, was a disappointment as 'he tore *The Furry Hand* to pieces.' But this didn't deter Freeman from contin-uing his work on the book, as later in 1915 he recorded that he had accepted Evans' condemnation of his first draft 'so meekly even so eagerly.' He vowed that one of his great tasks for 1916 would be to have in his possession a first-rate novel. AJF also regarded the redrafting and rewriting of his novel as a path of spiritual development, 'because quite apart from its results for my literary skill, it will train me in patience, carefulness, perseverance, sense of beauty, industry and will power.' He was also planning to submit to the publishers a 'dozen or more excellent short stories', five of which were already in draft or finished. There is only one more mention of his novel *The Furry Hand* when on New Year's Day 1917 he wrote that:

A year ago I was still novel writing and 'religionising'… but beginning better of both. The year has been valuable in clearing my mind. I must say I have given up novel writing and religion. I intend at any rate to finish The Furry Hand one day and I may write a social novel… but my views on writing and religion and things generally have taken a new shape.

One explanation for why he stopped writing in his diary can be seen in his intention to put 'all his best' into, and live for his work with the WEA. As he put it quite candidly:

> I have ceased to save my own soul… I've really found my way at last. All my Socialism and Religion are ending in this work for democratic education. It is the all important concern; my soul is in it; I am in many ways equipped for the task.

The Evolving Relationship with The Great School

Throughout the period from 1913-16 Freeman engaged himself yet more deeply with Richardson's *The Great Work* and recorded his personal and spiritual struggles for development. He placed great trust in this work and in his relationship with Herman Hille, from whom he seems to have derived much of his inspiration, not only in his personal but also in his professional life. As AJF progressed he found himself to be entering on a further phase in his work in The Great School 'and am gradually discovering more and more ultimately all the little cracks in my armour and (I hope) mending them.' Despite this, he increasingly felt the value of the work of the School and its potential contribution to his own life as well as the world at large. His sister Daisy, who visited him regularly in Sheffield, was also a convert to *The Great Work* and studied 'with unflagging perseverance' to qualify for 'studentship'.

However, this intensive work, coupled with his professional responsibilities, caused friction in his relationship with Nora and he often castigated himself for being weak, morally unsound or treating her in a too 'masterful' way, which often caused her to cry. For example, 'the problem of my moral status had occupied the only surplus energy I have had. I am convinced that I am shockingly weak-willed and shall take a long time to learn self-control. Sometimes I almost despair and wonder if I shall ever be good'. He also started to become impatient with his progress and notes that 'I must decide on some punishments for myself for failure to keep my resolutions' so he divided his day into 15-minute slots, with time for writing, time for study of *The Great Work*, making diary entries, meditating and praying. In addition to his reading of Richardson, he was also consulting books such as William James's *The Principles of Psychology*, and his strict personal regime was probably inspired by James's chapter on habit and the importance of keeping 'the faculty of effort alive in you by a little gratuitous exercise every day.'

Despite Freeman's concerns, his instructor Hille was pleased with his progress, and he often received notes from him with 'encouraging words'. One day he adds: 'And crashing into all these longings and endeavours comes a thunderbolt from Hille'. By this Arnold refers to his admission to the Ethical Section, on the condition that he dedicated three hours a day to his spiritual work.

The Great School was so structured that each student, after successfully passing each course, was evaluated by their Instructors, with advancement to the next course dependent upon the student's demonstration of consistent, intelligent effort, timely submission of lessons, understanding of the material, and correct attitude of soul. Freeman described it in the following way, which perhaps demonstrates his total commitment to the School and its work:

> This brings me to the first and greatest resolutions. I have been doing my work for the School latterly fairly well, but only fairly well. I have not been putting my very best into it and I don't feel that it has been influencing my daily life sufficiently. Now I have about another 20 topics to answer before I pass onto the next section of the work. (And I may say here incidentally that unless I can satisfy the School, I shall not be allowed to go on to the next section).

The ultimate aim of all this work was entry into the 'secret ethical section', and despite Sylvester West's unrelenting hostility towards Richardson, he is probably right in claiming that 'studying' *The Great Work*, and the eventual progression that resulted, required nothing more than a student memorising most of TK's works and then being tested by their instructor. West goes on to say that the real object of this 'secret ethical section' was no more than a bait for Richardson to sell his books and 'to hold and absorb the attention of his students, while he took their money'.

Given Freeman's strict commitment and undivided devotion to the work of the School, it becomes obvious when reading his diary entries that he certainly became (in West's words) a 'willing, abject, dogmatic and blind believer', who was trained to carry out the will of TK and his 'dishonest spirit guides, to whom he referred as the Great Masters.'

However, by mid-1916, Freeman, who had started to drift away from the guru's work, finally decided to give up his work as a student in The Great School. What led to this he tells us is a 'bitter ten minutes' he had with Nora. He was writing a paper for the School when Nora came in and asked what he was doing and showed her fierce displeasure that he was finding time for work of that sort:

> This studying of mine has been a constant cause of friction between us. She doesn't like it because it is secret; she has no share in it, because it brings me in intimate relationships with others, because it is a different form of selfishness.

Although he still believed in all the great principles that the School propagated he did give up his studies, without any intention of taking refuge in another faith, but only to throw himself into supporting his family and dedicating his working life to the WEA.

In 1916 Richardson was found by the trustees of The Great School to be addicted to heroin and was admitted to a Wisconsin sanatorium where he met, and later married, one of the nurses, Noneta Richardson. He and Noneta left the mid-west immediately after their marriage and moved to California, where he bought a mansion, probably with funds embezzled from The Great School. This caused a split in the movement between those who believed Richardson had never been a master and those who believed he had lost that status by his fraudulent activities. The Great School continued in California as The Great School of Natural Science, and published *Life in Action*, the journal founded by Richardson and Huntley, but in 2019 discontinued its activities.

The following diary entry dates from shortly prior to the fall of Richardson: 'TK does not impress me as a man of outstanding intellectual ability, therefore, I wager, he could never have formulated this philosophy himself'. Freeman does not doubt his character, but only his intellectual capacity. 'Sean Williams and I have felt this all along.' And in September 1916 Freeman declared, 'TK has fallen! Like a rat I deserted the sinking ship just at the right time'.

Thus ended Freeman's six-year relationship with Richardson and his 'Great School', which coincided with his decision to give up his dream of becoming a writer and to dedicate his professional life to being a good Tutorial Class Lecturer, even if it meant working for a lower salary than he received from the WEA. He was still committed through 'hard work' to make Sheffield the best-educated town in England... to write less in his dairies and to be less introspective and selfishly pious.

This required him to give his whole-hearted support to the WEA and its philosophy of 'democratic education'. Arnold believed that if he could contribute to making that institution sufficiently powerful in Sheffield it would stimulate all other branches to make great efforts. He did, however, feel the loss of Fisher who at this time had just been elected as a member of parliament for Sheffield Hallam and appointed as President of the Board of Education in Lloyd George's government. Freeman articulated their shared vision as follows: it was essential to educate 'the most influential of the labouring classes as on such education depends the whole future of this country... education is the most revolutionary force in existence. Set a man thinking and you have saved him. Stir him up! This is my creed henceforth.' At the start of 1917 Freeman again appears to have been 'settled' with his professional life. He believed he had 'found my way at last.'

Great Britain After the War

After this war there is coming the Great Reconstruction and I must play a part in it. People think I am a shirker in not fighting... education is the only thing that can save England and the world and Providence has granted me the priceless privilege of earning my livelihood in the most promising of movements for building up the Coming State. (Diary, January 1916).

In 1917 Lloyd George's government created the Ministry for Recon-struction to address a wide range of economic, social and political issues, including the improvement of industrial relations, the position of women in post war society, and the prevention of post war unemployment. There was also an increasing concern in government circles about the unrest in the 'industrial population' and the 'rise of a revolutionary spirit' among the workers. It was in this context that Sidney Webb and AJF published their 1916 pamphlet *Great Britain After the War*, asking questions about what would happen in regard to trade, employment, wages, prices, trade unionism and above all education. Although originally written as a guide for students, and dedicated to the WEA, it remains a useful mirror of socialist thinking on how the problems of a country recovering from a war could be solved. One of the top priorities was education, as it was believed that education could be a transformative force in the world:

> The subject to which above all others we desire to draw attention is that entitled: *Can we effect a Revolution in our system of Education?* We suggest that failure to find an affirmative answer to that question will mean the frustration of the national hope of effective recovery from the war, of building up a civilisation worth fighting for. Through education alone can the men and women of this country exercise, in fact, the political sovereignty which is as yet theirs only in name. Through education alone can we find a way to the beauty and order, the freedom and fellowship, the culture and joy, in the triumph of which, in the spirit of John Ruskin and William Morris, the leaders of the Workers Educational Association, rightly foresee: the Vindication of Democracy.

The pamphlet also predicted a more egalitarian society brought about by state intervention in the lives of poorer people. The Britain of the future, they argued, would be a finer country because the war would arouse us 'from our slothful acquiescence in the social iniquities that persist around us'. There are echoes of Freeman's work on *Boy Life and Labour* when the authors suggest that more money needed to be invested in education so that, for example, Elementary schooling became compulsory and full-time attendance was implemented for every boy and girl up to the age of fifteen. Any kind of wage-earning employment was to be made illegal and the physical wellbeing of the child made a primary consideration.

AJF's interest in education can be found earlier in his book *An Introduction to the Study of Social Problems*, (a second edition was published by the WEA in 1918), in which he presents his views on how best to reform the education system, arguing that 'education should enable the child to realise his oneness with mighty forces actively at work to enrich the life of humanity, it should release the child's spiritual energies, by psychologically appropriate appeals to his sense of wonder, of beauty and of idealism'. These ideas were discussed in greater depth in his next publication, written together with Frank Herbert Hayward.[32]

The Spiritual Foundations of Reconstruction

Frank Herbert Hayward (1872-1954) was a District Inspector of Schools for the London County Council, a supporter of the secularist movement and a founding member of the Moral Instruction League, which was set up to further ethical and civic teaching in schools on a non-theological basis. He shared in common with Freeman a desire to help working people in that he also worked tirelessly for thirty years for the cause of elementary education in the poorest districts of East London. Hayward says in his autobiographical reflections that when he made an acquaintance of Freeman's he was 'one of the few men actively on the lookout for an educational contribution to the very threatening contemporary situation'. Together, Freeman and Hayward co-authored the book, *The Spiritual Foundations of Reconstruction*, which addressed the perceived problems in the educational system and how in the 'after-war disorder and conflict', solutions might be found on how to 'spiritualise' the nation and bring about the fundamental reforms required 'to raise the intellectual and spiritual standard of the community'. Interest in the spiritualisation of education or moral education had been gaining ground in educational circles since the end of the nineteenth century with the likes of Michael Sadler and Frank Gould publishing books and pamphlets on moral instruction in schools and, especially in the aftermath of war, on education for peace, and social and spiritual reconstruction.

The basis for Hayward's view of education was derived from his lifelong interest in and study of Johann Friedrich Herbart (1776–1841), whose educational principles were based on *virtue* or the idea that the purpose of education is to strengthen the moral character of the child and to educate them for citizenship. As Hayward and Freeman point out in the first chapter of *The Spiritual Foundations of Reconstruction*:

> If our children are to grow up – not, as we have done, amid confusion and ugliness, but in an environment of order and loveliness – there must also be developed for the appreciation of this environment a widely diffused reverence for Beauty… after war, disorder and conflict can be avoided only if the minds of people are filled with such ideals of national and international citizenship as will assure unity and co-operation. (p.4)

They go on to say that:

> The function of the schools is to educate the community into a knowledge of Truth, a sense of Beauty, and a love of Goodness; that function they have failed to discharge.

In this publication it is less easy to discern the source of Freeman's educational outlook. The focus of the book is on the idea of 'Celebration' as a tool for moral and civic education and it is clear that the greater part of the writing stemmed from Hayward and was a precursor to his next book, *A First Book of School Celebrations*, published a year later. In this work Hayward reiterates in more detail what is found in *The Spiritual Foundations*, where he advocates the policy and practice of celebrations covering a wide field of topics, ranging from the prophetic utterances of holy men, bards, and seers, to the rise and fall of world conquerors and anniversary celebrations of great men. So it is difficult to ascertain with any concrete certainty the part that Freeman played in the writing of the book. The only reference in the diaries to the education of children is made on his visit to the Ruskin Home School at Heachem in June 1907, where he was enthused about the teaching and learning methods of Harry Lowerison; so it is worth questioning whether John Ruskin's educational philosophy influenced him in any way.

There is no direct reference to Ruskin in Freeman's diaries, but as mentioned above, he references Ruskin in his booklet *Great Britain After the War*. However, as Stuart Eagles points out, 'influence is a slippery term. Legacies and genealogies of ideas are difficult to trace.'[33] One definite fact we have is that his old friend and mentor John Clifford thought Ruskin a 'great prophet' and ran a Ruskin reading club at his home, where they read *The Crown of Olives*. We don't know whether AJF attended this club but given Clifford's influence on him it is a fair assumption that Clifford's sermons and addresses were infused with Ruskin's ideas, for example, on social justice, the education of women, and the improvement of conditions for the working classes. Moreover, Eagles also draws attention to the influence Ruskin had on the Labour movement, the Independent Labour Party and the Settlement Movement, all organisations that Freeman became involved with at different stages in his life. Freeman also shared Ruskin's interest in the education of the 'labouring' men and women and found the exploitation of the poor abhorrent. As we have seen above, AJF, like Ruskin, believed that life should be full of Truth, Beauty and Goodness, based upon a moral and ethical society. So we can definitely find social and political issues in Freeman's ideas that resonate with those of Ruskin.

One definite example of Ruskin's influence on Arnold's work is the idea of moral education, which, Ruskin argued, takes precedence over intellectual education and should be a 'morally transformative process in which the education of the soul matters more than practical education.'[34] Throughout the text of *The Spiritual Foundations* the authors contend that the most important element of the education is the soul development of the child rather than that of the intellect. Emphasis is placed on music, poetry and the enjoyment of 'moral art'. The authors also draw attention to the arts, crafts and other creative activities as serving a higher moral and social purpose, something that Ruskin strongly advocated in his lectures given to 'the workers and labourers of Great Britain' and later published in *Fors Clavigera*.

As Sara Atwood points out, 'Ruskin believed in active learning and his approach to teaching was dynamic. His main concern, in correspondence and books as well as in lectures, was to make his readers (or listeners) see clearly, to provide visual, tangible examples of the principles or subjects he taught.' Examples of such 'active learning' can be found in Hayward and Freeman's chapter on 'Mechanical Aids and Devices', where they suggest that instead of the 'often tattered charts of the Lord's Prayer', beautiful wall charts of 'Space and Time' could be placed on classroom walls. For example 'geographical maps, constructed on a more dignified principle than the present linen roll-ups' or 'Portraits of great men, simply framed and suitable for receiving wreaths of honour.'

In summary there is some agreement between Ruskin and the authors about the desire to have a holistic approach to education with the governing principle that all children should be taught 'what to admire, what to hope for, and what to love'. An example of this is found in the chapter on the Enrichment of Memory, where a scheme is proposed to supply the child with a 'vast supply of noble memories' through readings of the great poets such as Keats, Wordsworth, Shakespeare and others, such as Goethe and Dante, with the ultimate aim of binding people of different nations and cultures together 'to establish a common culture through memories bestowed in the schools.'

The Equipment of the Workers

An integral part of the period of reconstruction that followed the First World War was a growing demand for the provision of adult education. One of the research projects closely related to this was the survey conducted by Freeman: *The Equipment of the Workers*, started in 1917 and eventually published in 1919. Writing on New Year's Day 1917, Freeman remarked, 'we're getting the sanction of the Executive (WEA), for a most valuable investigation. This will be my Magnum Opus for the next 18 months or more.' He named himself, Lady Mabel Smith and Ballard, among others, as the 'Committee of Enquiry'. According to some commentators it was one of the most significant attempts to document the cultural milieu of the working classes in the early twentieth century.

Four hundred and eight women and four hundred and eight men were chosen to represent the manual workers of the city in order for researchers to obtain a picture of how the working class lived their lives, spent their free time, and felt about their role in society. Nearly all of the volunteers came from working class backgrounds, with railway workers, shop assistants and manual workers assisting Freeman, who collated and edited the results and presumably did most of the writing.

The survey was designed 'to cover all those individuals referred to by the rich as 'the workers', 'the toilers', 'the masses', 'the common people', 'the lower classes', 'the poor', 'the proletariat'. Based on data from interviews covering educational and political ideas, uses of leisure, musical tastes, aesthetic feelings, social and religious activities, and reading habits, the working classes were divided into three categories: 20 to 26 per-cent were considered intellectually 'well-equipped', 67 to 73 per-cent were 'inadequately-equipped', whilst 5 to 8 per-cent were deemed to be 'mal-equipped'. So-called 'well-equipped' workers were considered to consist of men and women who had been 'awakened to the seriousness and the splendour of existence'. They were active individuals who could cope with life and desired fine things; 'living for noble ends'. The researchers believed that within these awakened individuals, intellectual, moral and aesthetic elements mingled in varying proportions according to their unique constitution, enabling them to offer a positive spiritual value to the community.

Some of the interviewees were judged to be well-equipped on the grounds of being respectable and morally righteous, rather than because of their intellect. 'Inadequately equipped' workers, on the other hand, were defined as men and women whose distinguishing characteristic was that 'they are asleep… the mass of them let shameful slumber thrall them; they muddle through life; they are spiritually inert; they desire to rest and be left alone; they do not live for ends beyond immediate satisfactions; they are emphatically not "bad" people… but at present their value to the community is economic rather than spiritual, that of beasts of burden rather than that of free human beings.'

The least capable of the working classes were categorised as 'mal-equipped'. They were deemed to read 'nothing of any value', be possessed by 'root-desires' which were 'contemptible', and seek recreational pleasure through the likes of 'Football, Picture Palace, Music Hall and Public-Houses' (Freeman, 1919: 49). Moreover, 'their existence (so long as their defects remain uncured) is a positive evil for the community'; they are regarded as the 'rotters', the 'wastrels', the 'Yaboos'.

Unsurprisingly, it was the mal-equipped who were of particular concern and seen as the main targets for cultural reform. However, for Freeman, 'the fundamental solution' lay not in social reform per se but in a program of educational activities designed to develop good citizens whose skills and qualities met the needs of the local community; an idea that he explored further in his 1920 booklet, *Education Through Settlements*.

Education Through Settlements

Further signs of the influence of John Ruskin can be seen in Freeman's 1920s booklet, *Education Through Settlements*. As mentioned above, Stuart Eagles presents a convincing case for Ruskin's influence on the Settlement Movement, and a close reading of this booklet confirms, to a limited extent, Eagles' conclusions. For example, Ruskin argues in his essay *Unto This Last* that:

> The entire object of true education is to make people not merely do the right things, but to enjoy the right things, not merely industrious, but to love industry, not merely be learned, but to love knowledge, not merely pure but to love purity, not merely just but to hunger and thirst after justice.

So Ruskin's main principle and aim of education was the development of character, which included the qualities of truthfulness, humility, spiritual development, love of God, sympathy, charity, contentment, cheerfulness, good citizenship, the proper use of leisure time, and the development of good taste. These same themes are found throughout Freeman's small booklet. For example:

> To educate everybody is our object, to put into people such ideas as

will stir them to give the best of themselves to their jobs, to their homes, to their leisure activities, to their political service, to cause them to love their city so passionately that they will not be content unless it is as beautiful as they can make it. (p.16).

Approximately a year later Freeman set out the aims and objectives of the Sheffield Educational Settlement which echo Ruskin's utopian vision:

To establish in the City of Sheffield the Kingdom of God. The method is by education. By 'The Kingdom of God' is meant streets along which it is a pleasure to walk; homes worthy of the love of those who live in them; work places in which people enjoy working; public houses that are centres of educational and social life; cinemas that show elevating films; schools that would win the approval of Plato; churches made up of men and women indifferent to their own salvation; an environment in which people may have life and have it abundantly. By education is meant everything by means of which people may become more spiritual; books and pictures; solitary meditation and social intercourse; plays; celebrations and concerts; lectures, discussions and classes; everything that enriches human beings with that which described in three words, Beauty, Truth and Goodness, and described in one word is God.

By the time *The Equipment of the Workers* and *Education Through Settlements* had been published, AJF had already been appointed Warden of the Sheffield Educational Settlement. This is explored in the next chapter, but equally significant, and following on from his involvement with TK, was his 'rediscovery' of the work of Rudolf Steiner and his propagation of the Three-fold Social Order supported by a vision to build a new society.

Chapter Nine
Building a New Society

Rudolf Steiner, The Settlement and Controversy

In 1921 Freeman still had enough influence in Theosophical circles to be able to invite Annie Besant to lecture at the Settlement. Like him, Besant was asking questions about the threat to 'social democracy', how best to preserve the hard-won freedoms gained over the previous century and, above all, how to address the growing difficulties facing Britain in the aftermath of war. Besant's lecture was given in Montgomery Hall under the title, *The Reconstruction of the Shattered World*. Freeman obviously expected Besant to address some of these problems from an esoteric perspective and perhaps offer some new philosophical insights into the state of Britain. However, he found her lecture thoroughly underwhelming:

> As we went home in the taxi, I said to her: 'there wasn't much Theosophy in your lecture', (meaning there was nothing arising out of her philosophical outlook – which was the sort of thing I was looking for). She replied superiorly, 'It was all Theosophy'. But it wasn't. It was merely a rehash of the well-worn threadbare Socialistic shibboleths contributed by herself, Shaw, Webb and others to *Fabian Essays*.

This episode, as Freeman himself acknowledges, was the prelude to his 'rediscovery' of the work of Rudolf Steiner. He says in his booklet, '*Why I am a Steinerian*', that at that point in his life he felt that 'Baconian science' had not found the answer to the 'Riddle of the Universe' and he 'was altogether vague as to what the answer was.' Moreover, AJF 'had become disillusioned about the solution being presented by socialists of all descriptions to the Social Problem', a problem which he believed was more than merely a matter of economics and environment. Freeman's next key moment of discovery occurred shortly afterwards when he was thirty-five years old; an age at which, in Anthroposophical terms, people often experience a turning point in their lives, as it marks the beginning of the sixth seven-year biographical period. His own words best describe what happened at this point in his destiny:

> Very shortly afterwards I came across an article of Dr Steiner's in the Hibbert Journal. It was a translation of an essay that originally appeared in the *Soziale Zukunft* in Switzerland. It bore the bleak title, *Spiritual Life, Civil Rights, Industrial Economy*. This article made an immediate and profound impression on me. I underwent something like an instantaneous conversion. Here was a thinker altogether greater than the Shaws and the Webbs and the Wellses. Here was somebody who saw all round the social problem.[35]

It is interesting to consider why it was at precisely this point in his life that Freeman experienced a 'conversion' and also to question whether it was as 'instantaneous' as he claims. His journey from disillusionment to Anthroposophy, it seems, was more of a gradual process that took place over several years from about 1917 onwards. This slower 'conversion' is supported by remarks he made in the New Year of 1917:

> Reading the Guild Socialist literature and observing what State Socialism is meaning in this war and promises to mean afterward (specially in Lloyd George's vile hands) – I have become a Guild Socialist. I see it is the only thing that promises freedom and I became more and more a lover of liberty. Webbism is no ideal. Fabianism is played out.

It appears therefore, that before Arnold became acquainted with Steiner's ideas on the Threefold Commonwealth, he identified himself as a Guild Socialist and began to doubt the social reform agendas of Sidney and Beatrice Webb and the Fabian Society. Freeman is known to have worked

together with G.D.H. Cole
(1889-1959, known as the
intellectual leader of Guild
Socialism) on the 1916
WEA Yearbook. Moreover,
during the early years of the
Settlement, Freeman ran
classes comparing the
different political, economic
and social organisations of
the British State as
expounded by the Webbs,
Guild Socialism and
Steiner's Threefold
Commonwealth. A short
exploration of these ideas
derived from documentary
evidence from the
Settlement papers may

Rudolf Steiner, around 1905.

illustrate why, after a fifteen-year commitment to Fabian Socialism,
Freeman turned to Steiner to answer the questions he had been asking for
most of his adult life.

Competing Visions for Society

G.D.H. Cole was originally a member of the Fabian Society but gradually
became disenchanted with their programme, feeling that their state
socialist tactics ignored legitimate working-class concerns. After trying
unsuccessfully to persuade them to accept the Guild ideal, he resigned
but remained a member of the executive committee. Cole's vision of
Guild Socialism involved the complete social and political reorganisation
of society, such that power was transferred to professional guilds or self-
governing associations of producers. He argued that neither State
Socialism nor capitalism could fulfil the requirement of democracy
because neither could provide institutions through which active

citizenship might be achieved. As Cole pointed out, 'society will only be in health if it is in the full sense democratic and self-governing', and in his view this would involve active citizenship on the part of its members, mediated through Guilds. Fundamental to Cole's Guild Socialism was his argument that the essence of each individual human being was their unique individuality. His political theory, therefore, emphasized the priority of individual liberty over all other commitments; a philosophy that would have appealed to AJF, in contrast to the collectivism of the Webbs' organisational ideals.

Sidney and Beatrice Webb's *A Constitution for the Socialist Commonwealth of Great Britain* was published in 1920. Like the guildsmen, they were proponents of two parliaments, a political parliament and a social parliament, each with its own executive. But the social parliament would be a consumers' parliament instead of a producers' parliament. The two parliaments would be elected for fixed periods of ten years. The political parliament would handle the army, navy, foreign affairs, colonies, criminals and courts of justice. The social parliament would handle 'the mental and physical environment of the present generation', and would provide for the future of the community. Most importantly, the social parliament would control prices, taxes and wages, and the political parliament would have to apply for a budget to the social parliament for the army, navy, police and justice. Their plan aimed to safeguard personal freedom as the social parliament would give the citizen-consumers more control over nationalised industries. The Webbs sought to separate the coercive function of the sate from the economic.

By comparison, Steiner's theory of 'social three-folding' holds that society consists of three autonomous branches, the economic sphere, the political sphere, and the spiritual or cultural sphere. According to Steiner, these three realms are to be kept separate from one another, and each is subject to a different overarching principle: equality in the political realm, fraternity in the economic realm, and liberty in the cultural realm. Of these three, the cultural or spiritual sphere was paramount, and encompassed many of the activities and functions more commonly associated with the political sphere.

In his foreword to the 1921 edition of Steiner's book *The Threefold State*, AJF elaborates on this by saying that 'for reasons ascertainable by any reader who cares to set about discovering them, Dr Steiner insists that the human being, not in any vague mystical sense, is a spiritual being: fundamentally spiritual.' Freeman then goes into a little more detail, explaining that the 'Economic System' has to do with everything which is requisite for the human being's regulation of their material relations with the external world. Secondly, the 'Political or Equity System' deals with all that is made necessary in social life by the relations between humans, and thirdly, the 'Spiritual or Educational System' includes all that which proceeds from the individual and 'must of necessity find its way from the human personality, into the structure of the body social'.

To a general reader, Freeman's earlier works, which were examined in the previous chapter, might appear to be that of someone on an evangelical mission, but taking an Anthroposophical perspective, one could say that Freeman was driven by the impulses he brought with him into his destiny. In this interpretation his encounter with Rudolf Steiner's essay was the culmination of a long road of preparation to further the work of Anthroposophy within and beyond the boundaries of the Settlement. As Charles Davy writes about Freeman's 'discovery' of Steiner: 'Arnold had reached a goal in his pilgrimage, but not a resting place. It was more like a centre of operations. Henceforth his dominant purpose was to make Rudolf Steiner more widely known and appreciated'. He did this mainly by writing his concise booklets and organising lectures, seminars and workshops at the Settlement, but on a personal level his discovery of Anthroposophy slowly began to supply him with some answers to the questions he had been asking for most of his adult life.

For example, in his booklet *Rudolf Steiner's Message to Mankind*, Freeman writes that Alfred North Whitehead, one of the 'greatest of recent thinkers… insisted that if we are to have a full account of things, we shall have to supplement the recognised laboratory methods of investigation… with the imaginative insight of such poets as Wordsworth.' In other words, it is the method by which people investigate the material world that was important for Freeman; not surrendering the integrity of scientific knowledge but being able 'to advance to heights altogether beyond those "dreamable" to physical science.' It was Rudolf Steiner's 'spiritual science' that offered him a method and a way of looking at the world that went beyond the explanations of life and the universe given to him by a 'materialistically informed modern science.'

Freeman claimed that Steiner affirmed that in the course of their evolution it had now become right and proper for human beings to evolve super-sensible organs of cognition 'to gain their own direction of spiritual realities'. The 'occult' knowledge underlying this contends that all human beings, irrespective of their place in life, economic status or social or ethnic background, possess the ability to engage in self-transformation through regular esoteric exercises. Such 'occult knowledge' as Steiner points out in his *Knowledge of the Higher Worlds* is 'no more of a secret for the average human being than writing is a secret for one who has not learnt it… just as everyone who chooses the right way to set about it can learn to write, so everyone who seeks for the right path can become a pupil of occultism.'

The Anthroposophical approach to self-development claims not only to be for gaining access to the spirit but also for developing and enhancing our human qualities and virtues. Steiner, for example, encourages readers to develop their listening skills, their powers of observation, and to examine their prejudices while cultivating empathy for fellow human beings. Writing in the mid-1930s Freeman found that Anthroposophy was for him 'not an opiate, nor an intoxicant, nor even a grateful and comforting beverage,' but at first made things worse. However, after a time he began to master his 'own self' and found that without any 'sacrifice of one's intelligence and without any surrender of one's sense of humour, it is possible for a human being to bid farewell to that little, lower personal self of sensual cravings and childish fears and advance confidently towards a *Self* of understanding and creativeness and love.'

From his late teens onwards, AJF was already searching for answers to deep theological questions. In 1906 at the Keswick conference, although he underwent a 'religious conversion', he was still left in some doubt about his own religious convictions. In fact, by 1908 he called himself an 'agnostic', but later, it appears he took a similar stance to his hero George Bernard Shaw by refusing to place himself in any definable 'religious box'. Despite this, his questions about the nature of God and Christ and the Gospels remained with him during his social and educational work in both London and Sheffield. His study of Rudolf Steiner's writings on Christology began to provide him with answers, but not without difficulties. For example, in 1936 he writes:

> I found it exceedingly difficult to make an unprejudiced approach to what Dr Steiner had to say about Christianity. It was only after getting by many years of study his point of view about the universe in general that I found it possible to come to any hopeful understanding of his Christology.

Even for someone well versed in Anthroposophy, Steiner's lectures and writings on the Mystery of Christ and the Gospels are not easy to penetrate and understand. In his booklets AJF says that he 'might succeed in giving some clumsy interpretation of them... but he can only hint at the truth.'

It was the practical aspect of Steiner's teachings that drew Freeman deeper into the study of his lectures and writings and provided him, unlike his previous 'teachers' had, with a practical approach to achieving the Mastership he had longed for since his early twenties. But it was also the practical applications of Steiner's occult knowledge in fields such as biodynamic farming, medicine and education that Freeman worked hard to establish. The Settlement papers suggest that efforts were made in the mid-1920s to set up a biodynamic farm in the Sheffield area and, as we shall see later, a school based on Anthroposophical principles.

The Oxford Conference

Little has been written about the *Oxford Conference On Spiritual Values in Education and Social Life* held in Manchester College, Oxford from the 15th to the 29th of August 1922. What has been written, however, makes little mention of Arnold Freeman except for the fact that together with Professor Millicent Mackenzie he was joint Honorary Secretary.[36] The reason why this conference will be discussed here in some detail is

that despite little documentary evidence of Freeman's work on this conference, he nevertheless played a key role in its inception and organisation.

According to a letter written by George Adams to Miss Engert, the
secretary of the British Anthroposophical Society, the idea for the Oxford
conference was initially conceived in Dornach at the Teacher's Christmas
Course, held over the Christmas and New Year period 1921-1922. Several
members and visitors held meetings with Professor Mackenzie, who then
consulted Rudolf Steiner on his agreement and availability, and the
outcome was a conference to be held with the provisional title of *Education
as a Spiritual Art*. It was also agreed at these meetings that Steiner would
meet some prominent people, who would give talks and lectures at the
conference, and that Professor Mackenzie and Arnold Freeman would act
as Joint Honorary Secretaries to 'bring about the conference'. According to
AJF in an account he wrote for the Anthroposophical Newssheet:

> Professor Mackenzie and I concocted the Conference in Dornach
> at the end of the year 1921/1922. We appointed ourselves *Joint
> Secretaries* of that which we resolved to bring into existence
> during 1922.

He goes on to describe how they wrote a leaflet with the title of the conference, *Spiritual Values in Education and Social Life*, in the belief that in a
time of crisis in national and international affairs it was essential to further
society's understanding of the spiritual values underlying education and
social life. Given Freeman's background in social work and social research,
and his recent discovery of and interest in Steiner's idea of three-folding,
it can be safely assumed that he insisted that a consideration of that theme
be reflected in both the conference's title and content. In his opening
address, the Principal of Manchester College, L. P. Jacks, drew special
attention to Steiner's book *The Threefold State* by saying the main idea was
to disentangle political, economic and educational life from the 'confusion
into which they have fallen today, to disentangle without disrupting, to
deliver these three necessary functions from confusion and coordinate
them, to synthesise them on a higher level.' He then emphasised how
important a link education had with the social life and how it could not

properly be comprehended 'except in connection with the wider aspects of social life and the prevailing social conditions.' Again, it is not difficult to assume that Freeman had some input here as he mentions in his reminiscences that he met Jacks during the organisation of the conference and discussed for a long period the ideas of Steiner and Anthroposophy.

It is also useful when looking for evidence of Freeman's role in the organisation of the conference to examine the 'prominent people' who were invited to give papers or participate in some other way. Firstly, as discussed above, Freeman had very close contact, if not even friendship, with H. A. L. Fisher, who was appointed President of the conference but, because of his commitments as Minister of Education, could not attend and instead submitted a paper which was read out by L. P. Jacks. So, it is safe to assume that AJF was the motivating influence behind the invitation of Fisher and, given their connection, was probably tasked with inviting him. Other members of the general Committee had close links with Freeman as well. For example, John Mackenzie Mactavish was a member of the WEA, becoming its leader in 1916. Edmond Holmes who gave a paper at the conference entitled *The Function of Joy in Education*, was a member of the Theosophical Society and probably knew Freeman in that capacity, and it is possible that he was also known to Arnold's brother, Peter. A more definitive link can be made to Professor Gilbert Murray who knew AJF at Oxford where, in 1909, they discussed the future of socialism. Murray was a classical scholar and a close friend of Fisher who, before the First World War, had used his involvement with government to help those imprisoned as conscientious objectors. R. H. Tawney was another individual whom Freeman may have known from his work in the WEA and the University Extension movement. There is even a tentative link to John Drinkwater, whose plays were performed at the Settlement in Sheffield and whose play *X = O* was performed at Oxford.

In summary, it can be argued that Freeman played a leading role both in the organisation and in the content of the conference. He was probably quite happy to work 'behind the scenes' and let others stand in the limelight. The seeds planted at Oxford were carried further with the eventual founding of the Waldorf School movement in the UK.

Freeman and Mackenzie also participated in the New Ideals in Education conference at Westminster College, Cambridge, in 1928 where Millicent Mackenzie gave a lecture on 'Comenius: The Pioneer of International Education', and Freeman gave a lecture on Spiritual Values in Education.

The Settlement

The majority of the early Settlements were associated with universities or Oxbridge Colleges and fulfilled more of a social than an educational function.[37] For example, the founding of Toynbee Hall by Samuel and Henrietta Barnet was focussed on their vision to create a place for future leaders to live and work as volunteers in London's East End, bringing them face to face with poverty, and giving them the opportunity to develop practical solutions that they could take with them into national life. Educational Settlements, however, (the first was the Swarthmore Settlement in Leeds, founded in 1909), fulfilled more of a religious or spiritual endeavour and concentrated on the provision of adult education. These settlements gained the full support of the (Quaker) Rowntree family of York, emerging as they did out of a desire to embed adult education firmly in the localities and to provide educational opportunities for those who could not afford either the time or money to attend college or university.

The Settlement in Sheffield grew out of the Neighbourhood Guild Association (NGA): an association founded by the American social reformer Stanton George Coit, whose inspiration it was to unite local neighbourhoods and communities to 'carry out, or induce others to carry out all the reforms – domestic, industrial, educational, provident or recreative – which the social ideal demands.' Before the First World War the NGA had premises at the corner of Oxford Street and Shipton Street, which was used as a hostel for girls that was eventually purchased by the YMCA, who met the cost of converting the building. In 1918 A. E. Copson, the local YMCA secretary, invited Arnold Freeman to become warden of their newly acquired premises, to be named the Sheffield Educational Settlement. As we know from earlier chapters, Freeman's knowledge of literature and particularly drama was extensive. It was ideal then, that the programme of refurbishment included the creation of a small theatre, and

1951, Arnold outside the Settlement in Sheffield.
He often wore his old dressing gown embroidered by his sister, Dolly.

a Settlement Dramatic Society was established in order to prepare plays for performance. Freeman reflected on those early days in a short article in *Facts and Dreams,* 1924, in which he recalled the refurbishment of the Settlement:

> November six years ago (1918), found me in the thick of the noise and smell and dirt of bricklayers, plasterers, painters, joiners, plumbers and every other kind of builder's operatives, wrestling with the creation of the Settlement... there should be realised something beautiful at the corner of Shipton Street and Oxford Street... nothing was ordered ready made. It all grew. Things arose on the spot; spontaneous, seemly; organically appropriate. Development by development, the thing emerged. A live creature. I was proud of the result.

For Freeman, the building of the Hostel was his biggest concern at the time, 'it monopolised my energies in the early days', as it required extensive

reconstruction and furnishing, not to mention the matter of supplying all
the needs of future residents. It took six to eight months to bring the
Hostel in 'material manifestation, but completed it was the most beautiful
interior in the city.'

One of the many journalists who visited the Settlement was George
Follows, who later died in the Munich Air Disaster. In his article entitled,
The Philosopher of the Dark Streets he encapsulated what the Settlement
and the man who led it were all about:

> Only a man who was born there or Arnold Freeman, could love
> Shipton Street… Freeman is often there before the steel workers are
> out of bed and always leaves late at night… tea, cakes and billiards.
> Freeman kept the tea and cakes and moved out the billiards. It was
> all against experienced advice. Instead, he brought in arts, history,
> philosophy, drama, folk dancing, metaphysics. Labourers sat in a
> circle and discussed the glory that was Greece and in the tiny theatre
> took their parts in Oedipus Rex, Shakuntala and Hamlet. Freeman
> describes his job as helping people to find a philosophy of life.
> His big regret is that the businessmen already had a philosophy of
> their own… Today Freeman's elbows stick unapologetically out of
> his jacket sleeves. He bought the jacket thirty-five years ago in
> Oxford… to find his study one ducks through a hole in the wall.
> A door would cost £20. He thinks he is at a halfway house.

It seems it was possible in the space of one week to take part in arts, crafts,
walks, bake a cake and hear lectures on a range of subjects including
history, economics and literature. It is true that Freeman rose early, took
a cold bath and caught the very first tram into the city. It is true that one
had to duck through a hole in the wall to get to his office. He also threw
out the billiard table, but whether his elbows really stuck out of his jacket
sleeves is questionable, as are many of the other apocryphal stories told
about his dress, manner and personality.

*About 1950, Arnold and granddaughter Pearl on the stage of
the Little Theatre, Shipton Street, Sheffield.*

The Little Theatre

At the heart of the Settlement's activities was the 'Little Theatre', as it was affectionately known as, and despite its small size Freeman was very ambitious in his choice of plays, producing, for example, such works as Goethe's *Faust I and II* and Schiller's *Mary Stuart*.[38] The stage was only two feet off the ground, backstage accommodation was minimal, but there was seating for an audience of 150. The theatre, together with an amateur dramatic society, existed before Freeman became Warden. He continued a tradition of staging the dramatic arts and was able to follow his own belief in the importance and significance of drama for the social, cultural and spiritual life of the community. Writing in 1919, he reflected that the production of a play is 'the supremely educational thing' and 'might be perhaps regarded as the consummation of the activities of the Settlement'.

Drama, therefore, became a vital part of the educational work of
the Settlement. The plays were chosen with care, but it wasn't just the end
product that was important. Everything about the process of preparing
for a production; choosing and making the costumes, scenery, music, and
the historical and social context within which the play was set were integral
to what Freeman saw as a complete educational experience. To help people
immerse themselves in all aspects of a play, he would put on classes to
study the play and its context. Sometimes the production of a play arose
from an existing series of lectures. Costumes, scenery and music were all
carefully researched, and where possible, were provided in-house.

In the early days of the theatre, which went under the name of the
St. Philip's Settlement Dramatic Society, Freeman worked closely together
with Herbert and Marion Prentice, who both started their careers at the
Settlement. Harold Ridge, another individual who later became renowned
for his stage lighting, also worked together with the Prentices. In these
early years it is not known how much Freeman was actually involved in the
production of the plays, although it is possible to speculate that his close
working relationship with Prentice and Ridge gave him the tools to
produce the plays when Prentice moved on in 1923.[39]

The very first play to be produced at the Settlement by the amateur
dramatic society was Tolstoy's, *Where God Is, Love Is*, when the Prentices
were residents at the Settlement, though the very first play Prentice
produced was John Galsworthy's *Silver Box* in 1919, with his wife Marion
taking the role as Mrs Jones the charwoman. A report in the Sheffield
Independent commented on her 'first rate acting' which touched 'a really
high level'. 'Few of our repertory theatres can produce an actress more
faithfully portraying a curious admixture of virtue coupled with timid
and pathetic docility which characterises this part.'

Prentice produced and directed all of the plays, with Marion taking
many leading roles, and 1921 saw the first official meeting and founding
of the Sheffield Repertory Company, with affiliation to the British Drama
League. The Prentices continued at the Little Theatre until 1924 when they
branched out independently and rented new premises at the South Street
Schoolroom in Eldon Street, thus becoming independent of the Settlement

and founding the first permanent home of the Sheffield Repertory Company. They still maintained their connection with the Little Theatre, but this was entirely severed when they acquired their own permanent premises and moved to the former Temperance Hall in Townhead Street. Prentice eventually had a successful career in theatre, and later, television. For example, in 1932 he was appointed producer, by Sir Barry Jackson, of the Birmingham Repertory Theatre, and in 1946 he directed William Shakespeare's play, *As You Like It*, in the Stratford Theatre Festival at the Shakespeare Memorial Theatre in Stratford. He also directed two TV movies and dramatized *Alice's Adventures in Wonderland*, which was broadcast on BBC children's television on Sunday 1ˢᵗ January 1956.

It is possible to assume that Freeman took over the sole responsibility for the production of plays when the Prentices left in 1924, and by the time of his retirement he had successfully produced one hundred different plays which received wide acclaim in both the local and national press. Whilst Freeman's approach to producing a play is probably not unique, his underlying inspiration was to create a community spirit where everyone played a significant role irrespective of their abilities. Using an analogy from his footballing days, Arnold once wrote that it was very bad to concentrate purely on one's own part, much like dribbling a football and not passing it on to the other players. 'The more you feel your own part as if you were a finger in the whole human body, the better you'll act, the more helpful you'll be'. Actors were also discouraged from learning their lines prematurely so as to maintain the wholeness of the production. There was much more to these productions than the acting: settings, properties, lighting, costumes, publicity, selling tickets, and even helping with washing-up. A report written by Herbert Prentice in the *Sheffield Evening Telegraph* reveals more about the secret of the Little Theatre's success. For instance, the players spent months working on each production, reading and re-reading the play, discussing their characters, their characters' lives, and generally adopting 'their being, for the time in the atmosphere of the play'.[40]

Further reports from the press demonstrate the high quality of the productions. For example, *The Times* theatre correspondent often praised the company for its ambition:

Which is only equalled by its modesty… there are two most unusual things about the Little Theatre that have always appealed to me, and they are the two things that give the Little Theatre its unique quality. First, it is concerned wholly with good plays and not at all with box office *pull*. Profit making is never an influence in the choice it makes of what play to perform. Second, the players are not concerned in building up a popularity as individuals. They recognise that persons don't essentially matter; who takes this or that part is unimportant; so long as they were properly chosen, the job well done and the whole cast worked together to achieve it. With these two fine qualities we find a body of ordinary people virtually becoming transfigured in the acting of a drama that we should have thought was completely beyond them.

In December 1952 the *Manchester Guardian* commented favourably about the double bill *The Prometheus* by Aeschylus, coupled with a play from the Wakefield Cycle:

There can be few players in the country working consistently at such an elevation as those of the Sheffield Little Theatre. At a time when the general movement is all the other way, their urge seems to be to climb on into an ever rarer atmosphere; and they deserve the earnest (if somewhat awe-stricken) thanks of us all for keeping at least one corner of our theatre safe from triviality, smartness and self-admiration.

Freeman also wrote his own plays. In an article based on an interview with him, a reporter from the *South Yorkshire Times* and *Mexborough & Swinton Times* wrote that Freeman's play *Where Plato Learned His Lessons in Platonic Love* was an attempt 'to show that the best antidote to the growing influence of the totalitarian state is a return to the Greek ideals of love, fellowship and beauty.' Freeman argued that 'Greek Philosophy has a message for the modern world, and to show this he has taken passages from the teachings of Socrates, and has linked them, to form a dramatic sequence', by forging 'a link between the needs of the present day and the renaissance brought about in an earlier period by Greek philosophy and thought.' When the world most needed renewal, the play suggests, it turned to the Greek ideal as set by Socrates. 'With the modern trend of the world, great good might be found by getting back to his thought'.

Another play from the pen of Freeman is *Malvolio's Revenge*, which, true to his enjoyment of practical jokes, he initially promoted as a long-lost sequel to Shakespeare's *Twelfth Night*, based on a tradition that Shakespeare wrote some trifling sequel to *Twelfth Night*, and that in 1937 an academic working in the Bodleian Library came across a manuscript which he declared to be the missing play. This proved, however, to be false, despite some critics asserting it to be a genuine Shakespeare. Freeman did eventually confess to be the author of the work and said that he deliberately tried to write it in the way Shakespeare would have written it. Freeman also expressed his concerns that a number of friends who rang up to say how excited they were at the prospect of being present at a Shakespeare first night would be disappointed when they found out he was the author.

The 1923 General Election

In the December 1923 General Election, Freeman became the Labour candidate for the Hallam division of Sheffield, causing much controversy within the Settlement and giving his opponents the opportunity to attack him for splitting the anti-conservative vote. On 16th November 1923 in a general letter, very likely written to all members of the Settlement, Freeman stated his motivations for putting himself forward as a candidate:

> With the utmost intensity of personal conviction it seemed to me that the Crisis in Human Affairs demanded of this Settlement an experiment in Christianity. I regard my participation in this election and my entry, if elected to the House of Commons, as a phase of that Experiment. I feel I am under a sacred pledge to those who have all helped to build up this institution to keep inviolate, in my own person and in this election, and, if it comes, in the subsequent phase in parliament, the principles which our Settlement is striving

to exemplify and propagate. I regard the fight as a crusade rather than a campaign.

Just over a week later he wrote a letter to the *Sheffield Daily Telegraph* that illustrates the amount of opposition he faced by entering this election. To take the sting out of it, however, he adds a portion of classic Freeman humour:

> Numerous statements keep appearing about me in your paper, some of them editorial, some of them in the press and correspondence columns. And I am similarly honoured in the three other local papers. I don't at all complain, but I ask for the opportunity to point out that if I attempted to keep up with all these statements, I should certainly do nothing else between now and polling day. When the election is over I trust you will allow me several columns of your space to deal in detail with everything that has been said about me in your paper during the election. Meantime I must leave your staff and correspondents to gnash their teeth over the fact that there are only 10 Commandments for me to break.
>
> (28th November 1923).

He eventually came second, with the Unionist candidate in first place and the Liberal on a narrow margin third. Exactly how Freeman thought that by becoming a politician he could make significant social, educational or political changes is hard to say. He argued that all his life he had been a champion of the 'mass of the people', but as a politician he would remain impartial, and he would fight without giving any pledges or promises. Apart from an offer in 1928 from the North Leeds constituency to be Labour candidate, he never entered the political arena again.

Facing Hardship

In 1924, the settlement was facing financial problems, which resulted in the sale of the hostel and the end of the residential component of the business. Although the sale cleared the debts, it was necessary to reduce Freeman's salary from £450 to £400 a year. In addition to this, his devotion and continued propagation of Anthroposophical ideas instigated an unsuccess-ful attempt to remove him from the wardenship. With the support of his faithful co-worker, Doris Violet Barber, he continued in the post.

The attempted coup to oust Freeman from his position as warden revolved around the issue of 'democratic control' of the Settlement, but it came to a critical point when the Educational Settlements Association, to which the Settlement was affiliated and from which it received funding, was threatening to withdraw its financial support because Freeman allowed a Communist Sunday School to hold its meetings at the Settlement.[41] A further issue that raised concerns for some Settlement members and the ESA was Freeman's politics. Some of the Settlement Council members resigned, with one accusing Freeman of propagating socialist propaganda. Both the ESA and his own Committee were also voicing their concerns over his adherence to Rudolf Steiner and Anthroposophy. There were crit-icisms of the content of what he taught and his inclination 'to follow the latest strange theories of Continental philosophers and savants'. In 1925, after his return from a holiday in Greece, there was an attempt to oust him from his leadership position. The Committee met to vote on Freeman's future with eight votes for his removal and eight against. Freeman used his casting vote which resulted in the resignation of the eight who voted in favour of ousting him and Freeman remained as warden.

Given Freeman's background and commitment to 'social democracy' it is surprising he declared that he would not run the Settlement democratically, as for him it was not about democracy but leadership. By this point the ESA had withdrawn its funding and disaffil-iated the Settlement, thus leaving Freeman and his loyal workers with the task of raising funds from other sources. Moreover, the ESA publicly withdrew their support from Freeman's previous and present policies, which probably motivated him to write a new 'democratic' constitution, giving students more control over how the Settlement was run. This didn't deter Freeman, however, from retaining control as, according to his prin-ciples, it was not possible to work in freedom on a democratic basis.

In a letter to all members of the Settlement dated 29th May, Freeman confessed that he was aware of his own limitations with regard to those who criticised his wardenship but appealed to 'to those who have supported me as well as those who are disaffected… to put into practical operation the Settlement idea'. It was imperative, he continued, to maintain in the City of Sheffield a 'centre of free spiritual life, where poor people can have some share in culture.' He then outlined the extreme financial difficulties they were facing with no public funds and their reliance on subscriptions, donations and any money they could collect from the theatre and other activities.

In the minutes of a meeting of the Finance Committee from July 23rd, 1925, suggestions were put forward on how to alleviate the financial crisis, one of which was to lower Freeman's salary down to £350 for a period of eight or nine months or longer if required. It was also stated that the Management Committee were under a 'moral obligation' to carry on the Settlement 'until this became financially impossible to be interpreted as the inability to meet the demands of the trades people or to pay the Warden a reasonable salary.' Moreover, Freeman was encouraged to 'secure paid work outside the Settlement' which would not prevent him from effectively discharging his duties as Warden. According to Grace Hoy, Freeman did return to work part-time for the University Extension movement and remained working there until his retirement in 1955.

Despite his difficulties, Freeman, together with his 'loyal supporters', was determined to continue with the work, and in 1928 a 'Craft-work' scheme was set up to help the unemployed of Sheffield. In the draft proposal, published in April of that year, it stated that only those who were unemployed and who had been members of the settlement for two years would be allowed to take part. Initially thought of as a training scheme where the unemployed could continue to draw their unemployment allowance or poor relief, it eventually became a 'branch' of the settlement. The craftwork produced was sold, for example at the Christmas Fair, or pieces were even made to commission, 'the sort of job it is often difficult to get done elsewhere'. The philosophy behind such a scheme was to enable individuals to create things of beauty, 'things which owe their appeal to structure and inherent design rather than to inartistically superimposed ornament and at the same time to learn the value of cooperative effort.'

Freeman also suffered bouts of nervous exhaustion during his time at the Settlement, and he tells us that in the winter season of 1934 he felt 'so worried, so nervously exhausted, so *done*,' that he made up his mind to give up lecturing. Despite this, he carried on for a few more weeks, until he found himself in the Sheffield Royal Infirmary, 'as a result, I believe, of these inner stresses.' He spent ten days in hospital which were for him 'festival moments' because he was 'free of all feelings of turpitude for not doing anything and made a full recovery with the help of Anthroposophical medicine and reading Steiner's *The Philosophy of Spiritual Activity*'.

In the years leading up to the Second World War it is possible to see from the Settlement's Monthly Leaflets, which Freeman edited and regularly contributed to, that he was acutely aware of the growing threat of Hitler's Germany, but was puzzled as to what attitude one should take. In preparation for a lecture he was to give he reproduced, in the March 1936 edition, a letter he wrote to some leading individuals of the day and asked them 'the fundamental question: What attitude ought we in this country to take up towards Germany?' He acknowledged that re-armament would not solve the problem, so he asked these individuals what they felt to be the right policy. Freeman received answers that varied in their approach, but most agreed that re-armament was not the answer and that the League of Nations needed a thorough revision of their Covenant. As John Atkinson Hobson (1858-1940), one of the leading economists and an apparently astute observer of current affairs wrote to Freeman:

> If there existed a strong genuinely international feeling among League members, the German menace could scarcely mature into a definite policy. But seeing that the League dared not challenge her re-armament, in defiance of the Treaty (Versailles), Germany is pretty certain to take early action in the Rhineland, or in Austria or on her Russian frontiers and then comes the critical test.

Later, in the March 1938 Monthly Leaflet, Freeman looked for a solvent to the 'World Crisis' in Rudolf Steiner's 'Threefold Commonwealth'. 'Certain things', he says, 'have now become necessary for the continued existence of civilised life: world economy, social equality and individual freedom.' He goes on to suggest that 'what is taking place around us is but the externalisation of an apocalyptic inner struggle,' which could only be solved if people brought to an end 'possessiveness and prejudice, overcome our obsession with the materialistic and the sense perceptible, acquire spiritual faculty and discover the Light of the World within us.'

In another article, entitled 'The Task of the English Speaking People', published in 1941 when the war was already underway, Freeman elaborates on the idea that this war and that of 1914-1918 arose 'inevitably out of the conditions of modern civilisation,' and one way out of the catastrophe would be to try new political and social systems. War, now and in the future, is inevitable between states, he argued, if each state continued to set up its own military frontiers, its own tariff barriers, and its own psychology of nationalistic exclusiveness. The way forward, he believed, was to cultivate 'inner relationships' in a community of nations on the basis of a threefold social order, but Freeman's voice was not heard and he, his family and his colleagues at the Settlement went on to experience another four years of war.

Helen Rootham

It is worthwhile spending some time on the life and personality of Helen Rootham. Firstly, because she was closely involved in the work at the Settlement, and secondly, because of her influence on her closest companion Edith Sitwell (who later became a renowned poet) to whom she was appointed governess in 1902.[42] Rootham was an experienced and talented musician besides being an aspiring poet, and it is suggested that 'she brought a fervour for the arts that would transform Sitwell's life... she would not have gone beyond talent to expertise in either poetry or music.' That Helen was positively influencing Sitwell's talent is found in letters she wrote to Sir George Sitwell during a stay Berlin in 1905. Rootham requested that Edith receive extra music lessons, preferably from a teacher in the 'German School', as she had a considerable talent and could achieve a professional standard. Richard Greene suggests that in the two letters she wrote to Sir George from Berlin, Rootham reveals much of 'Helen's personality: intensely ambitious, generous, hot tempered, self-dramatizing; honest to a fault.'

In 1913, the two women left the Sitwell family home and lived for a time in a rooming house at 14, Pitt Street in Kensington run by a Miss Fussell. It was only later in May 1914 that they moved to a flat in Pembridge Mansions, Bayswater. In 1927, Sitwell fell in love with the gay Russian painter Pavel Tchelitchew. The relationship lasted until 1928, the same year that Rootham underwent operations for cancer. Edith moved to Paris in 1932 with the terminally ill Rootham, to live with Rootham's younger sister, Evelyn Wiel, and she remained there until her companion's death in 1938.

In a short article in one of the 1938 Monthly Leaflets, Freeman remembered Helen Rootham and how she had discovered Rudolf Steiner and Anthroposophy through attendance at the Settlement:

> It was almost on her first visit to this settlement that Helen Rootham repeated some gossip she had heard to the detriment of Rudolf Steiner. She subsequently took down from our shelves in the Quiet Room his *Knowledge of the Higher Worlds* and something she read called up in her the reproachful question: What have I done? What right have I to repeat such things? Penitentially (sic) she set to work to study Rudolf Steiner's writings. And she became an anthroposophist – though she never ceased to be a devout catholic.

In 1934 the Settlement received a letter from Rootham stating that she wished to take a room in Sheffield 'for three months and work with the choir… I have really glorious plans… a Bach programme which would mean bringing in the Folk Dancers and necessitate a number of people learning to play pipes and flutes… but I know that it cannot be before 1935. But will they remember me? All this is a dream of course, but if I dream hard enough it may come true'.

Some years later Edith Sitwell was sitting on a couch in Hollywood talking to Marilyn Monroe when the conversation turned towards Anthroposophy:

We talked mainly as far as I remember, about Rudolf Steiner, whose works (Monroe) had just been reading. At one time Helen Rootham was most interested in Steiner, with the result that I found myself, one evening, watching what I believe was a Nature-Dance (something uniting one, I expect, with Mother Earth) in which ladies of only too certain an age galloped with large bare dusty feet over an uncarpeted floor. I do not know that this exhibition could be ascribed to Dr Steiner but it seemed to have something to do with Higher Thought, and I am afraid that Miss Monroe and I could not resist laughing.

Although tentative, it is possible to detect a thread weaving from Arnold Freeman's Settlement to Marilyn Monroe. There is now conclusive evidence that Monroe was reading Steiner and was introduced to Steiner's writings and lectures by her drama teacher, Michael Chekhov (1890-1955), nephew of the playwright Anton.[43] If not for the influence of Helen Rootham, Edith Sitwell would probably never have had the opportunity to discuss with Marilyn Monroe the ideas of Rudolf Steiner which according to Richard Greene had quite some 'impact on her poetry'.

The story of Helen Rootham is one of the very few that exists of an individual who was influenced by the work of Arnold Freeman in Sheffield and is supported by documentary evidence. As we have seen, thousands of people, including artists, academics, musicians, writers and poets (including Arthur Conan Doyle (1859-1930), and the Sheffield born Labour politician Roy Hattersley (born 1932), visited the Settlement and carried away with them fond and lasting memories of AJF and his team of workers.

Chapter Ten
War, Refugees and Retirement

The Second World War and The Sheffield Blitz

The worst nights for anyone living in Sheffield in 1940 were from December 12th to the 16th, when Hitler's Luftwaffe put their Crucible Operation into action and bombed the residential and industrial areas of the city. Sheffield was a principal target as it was a major producer of steel and armaments what with the English Steel Corporation's Vickers Works, which manufactured Rolls-Royce Merlin crankshafts for the Spitfire and Hurricane aircraft, and other key components for tanks, side and deck armour for warships, bomb castings and components for seventeen-pound anti-tanks guns.

Over 330 German aircraft are believed to have attacked the city and almost 700 people were killed, and approximately 82,000 houses were damaged or destroyed. Helen Shepherd tells us that on the night of 12th December 'the biggest tragedy occurred just before midnight when the Marples Hotel received a direct hit. The explosion caused the seven-story building to collapse into a pile of rubble, burying around 80 people who had been sheltering in the cellar. Only seven people were brought out alive; a number of victims were never recovered.'[44]

Grace Hoy reports that one night, when Adam Bittleston, a Christian Community priest, was giving a WEA lecture, 'the Settlement was caught up in one of the heavy bombing raids on the city. All squeezed into the little shelter built into the hillside garden at the side of the theatre', with Freeman taking his turn in acting as a fire warden. She recalls how with the outbreak of war a new phase of life began at the Settlement and brought with it new difficulties. Many people came who had mental or other difficulties seeking assistance. The difficulties of dealing with this change was exacerbated by travel restrictions, bombing, blackouts and rationing. A canteen was opened by Doris Barber and Cristina Stone which they managed to keep open throughout the war with a constant supply of good meals at a reasonable price. The canteen served meat, and as Freeman was a vegetarian and his office was above the kitchen, he had to endure the noise and bustle and, above all, the smell of meat.

Supporting Refugees

Both Arnold and Nora were very active in their support for refugees from Nazi Germany and other Nazi occupied countries in Europe. They both supported the peace movement and Nora represented the Educational Settlement in the work of the Sheffield Peace Council. Arnold was the chairman of the executive committee of the Sheffield Co-ordinating Committee for Refugees, with Rabbi Barnet and the Archdeacon of Sheffield as Vice-Presidents. This was renamed in 1941 the Sheffield Council for Refugees. The site at Hollowford was used as housing for refugees, as was a house in Bradwell on the other side of the valley. In 1939, in a notice from Freeman to the members of the Settlement, he made a direct appeal to help house thirty more Czech refugees. The *Sheffield Evening Telegraph* from March 1939 contains an article stating that thirty Czech refugees had arrived at Ham Hall, the model hostel at Dovedale, and that four others had already been installed at the Sheffield Educational Settlement's hostel at Hollowford, Castleton.

> Mr Arnold Freeman, the warden of the Sheffield Educational Settlement, told *The Star* today that an urgent appeal to take more refugees had been responded to and 15 more will find shelter at Hollowford and others will be housed at Sheffield's own hostel at Ravenstor, at Millers Dale, and at Derwent. Mr F. Turton, chairman of the Sheffield Youth Hostel Association, said: The Czech refugees are welcome to all the hospitality that is available at our hostels.

The Freeman family gave direct support to Astrid, Anita and Manfred Zydower, and all three lived with the Freemans in their early years in Sheffield. The older brother, Manfred, was eleven and he and his sisters Astrid and Anita, aged nine and ten, came to England in July 1939. Anita offered the following story at a conference in 2008 *Commemorating the Kindertransport*:

> We left Berlin saying goodbye to our parents to travel to England with the Kindertransport, hoping our parents would follow us, but, unfortunately, this was not to happen. My parents survived as far as we have been told until the summer of 1944 [*sic*], but were then taken away where as far as we know they died. My parents owned a shoe and clothes shop, but the shop was pulled down before our very eyes, and from that day life was never to be the same again, and our lives changed completely. We were met and saved by an elderly lady, Mrs Freeman, on Liverpool Street Station, who had initially said she would only take my sister and myself, but when she saw my brother holding our hands tightly she could not part us and took the three of us to her house in Sheffield. Mrs Freeman's own children were all at different universities at the time, and two of her children could speak some German which was very helpful. The Freeman family saw us through school and college, and my sister Astrid won a scholarship to the Royal College of Art in London, and became a famous sculptress and artist, who sadly died in 2005 at the age of 75.
>
> To us, Mrs Freeman seemed one of those rare human beings whose sense of goodness and wanting to help those in need made one feel there was some hope for mankind against a vast sea of evil. Writing and remembering the past has brought back so many feelings we had at the time, but we were fortunate that we had the chance to start a new life in England, sadly, of course, without our beloved parents.

Little is recorded about Anita, the middle child, but Manfred enrolled on a course in 1943 validated by the British Institute of Engineering Technology to train in radio servicing. He subsequently attended Camborne Technical

1951, Astrid Zydower at Clarendon Road, Sheffield.

1951, Anita Zydower at Clarendon Road, Sheffield.

1951, Astrid Zydower in Sheffield.
She went to Sheffield School of Art.

College in October 1944 and briefly lived with AJF's son Peter at Carbis Bay in Cornwall. He completed the course and returned to Sheffield in 1946. There is some correspondence in the SES papers about the funding of this course, and the Sheffield Council for Refugees gave him a small grant of ten shillings per week for twelve weeks to cover some of the costs. There is, however, much more biographical information available on Astrid who, as Anita points out, became a famous sculptress whose artistic life is documented in *Astrid Zydower – Her Life & Works* by Peter Amsden.

The three children were born in a small village in a part of Germany that is now Poland. One of Astrid's earliest childhood memories was the

sight of their once-friendly Christian neighbours emerging from Sunday
service to spit on her and her fellow Jews. After their transportation to
Sheffield they never saw their parents again who died in Auschwitz in 1942.

It is not clear how many refugee children the Freemans supported, but
in the archive, there is a letter from 1943 about a certain Lotte Frankenstein
and AJF wrote that he had 'taken five young refugees into my household and
during these last six years given an immense amount of time to refugee work'.
In one pamphlet distributed throughout the local community, he appealed
for help to find a home for 'three Jewish boys', two aged thirteen and one
aged fourteen. The financial side of supporting the children, and especially
providing them with education and training, appears to have been very
difficult. The Freeman family personally supported some of the children
(with help from AJF's mother), and sometimes they tried to gain support
from the Refugee Children's Movement, the body which organized the
Kindertransport. The local authorities were not always sympathetic, and
sometimes responded by questioning why they should support a German
girl beyond school leaving age, when an English girl had to go out to work.
The Sheffield High School for Girls was, however, more sympathetic when
they waived the fees for at least one of the girls. The Sheffield Council for
Refugees also gave some support.

The Post-War World

Since approximately 1944, Arnold Freeman had been asking Karl König to
come to Sheffield to lecture on his schools and his work with 'children in
need of special care'.[45] Eventually in May 1945 the first König Week took
place in Sheffield with lectures and workshops at the Settlement, where
Freeman had served as Warden since 1918. A public lecture was held on
Thursday 10th May in the City Memorial Hall entitled: 'The Camphill
Rudolf Steiner Schools for Children in Need of Special Care'. With his
typical enthusiasm, Freeman invited more than 300 people to listen to
König, among them some of the leading civic dignitaries and education-
alists of Sheffield. The lecture was also widely advertised in the Sheffield
newspapers. The next day, König, in his lecture at the Settlement, spoke on
'Rudolf Steiner's Significance for Our Age'. It is apparent from this event

that both men were already planning another visit for König the following year. König spoke warmly about his experience of Sheffield, saying that as he walked through the town that morning, 'I saw people and met people and found them extremely friendly'. He also had private conversations with Sheffield's Medical School Officer and the Director of Education who, he said, were 'stirred' by what he had to say about his work with children.

It was very likely during the second 'König Week' in 1946 that König suggested to Freeman the possibility of starting a school in the Sheffield area. In the early 1940s König travelled around Britain lecturing and meeting teachers to explore the possibility of opening schools for children in need of special care based on the ideas of Rudolf Steiner. His venture in Scotland was expanding from the small group that had first started at Kirkton House, near Aberdeen. The expansion included the purchase of Murtle Estate in April 1944 and later, in May 1945, Newton-Dee Village an establishment for boys in need of special care, all made possible by a gift from the Macmillan Family. As König stated in his 1945 lecture 'I could imagine if 20 or 30 people really try to start this work and carry on throughout the year, it could be a great, great spiritual success'. He planned to organize other such weeks in Glasgow and Perth and mentioned the possibility of working together with Freeman and others to bring about the founding of a school in Sheffield.

From the Settlement archives it is possible to see that from this point onwards Freeman began a desperate search for a suitable property to begin the school. In the summer of 1946 Freeman and some members of the Settlement Council visited König at Bieldside, near Aberdeen, where the founding of a school was discussed and where Freeman also spoke to König about a proposed periodical he was planning.

In the autumn of 1946 Freeman discovered Whitley Hall, a stately house near Grenoside to the north of Sheffield. It was a very run down property owned at the time by Captain Bingley, a retired army officer. Whitley Hall was used as an army headquarters during WWII, and at the beginning of the nineteenth century had been an academy 'for the sons of gentlemen'. In December 1946, after a lengthy correspondence with the owner, Freeman invited König to view the property, but he expressed his

*1951, Astrid Zydower, Nora White and Anita Zydower
with Brock the dog at Clarendon Road, Sheffield.*

doubts as to whether it was suitable for a school. He thought the £5,000 or
£6,000 that needed to be spent on it wouldn't be worth the investment,
and he doubted whether the required permits to run a school would be
granted. Much to Freeman's disappointment the idea was postponed.
In a letter dated March 1947 Freeman wrote the following to König:

> When you first suggested that we should start a 'König School' I feel
> it was a true inspiration. I do not think, however, that we under-
> stood the true implications of it… you were to have the ultimate
> responsibility as medical advisor. I rather had the idea, perhaps
> unjustifiably, that you were going to find the money. It was all too
> rash, too ill advised, too sudden.

Freeman did, however, remain committed to the idea of starting a school
in Sheffield and, philosophically, they both shared a vision of a future
social and cultural life built around the idea of community. The whole
of König's curative work with children was not an end in itself but a

means to establish residential communities based on the spirit of Rudolf Steiner's teaching. Freeman's vision was to build communities or new 'Anthroposophical Islands'. As he stated in this letter, a 'König School' in Sheffield would have a 'thick periphery of community all about it.' Without this he thought a school couldn't possibly succeed.

Freeman became increasingly fixated on what he called a 'König-School-Anthroposophical-Community-Project'. He stated that he had no particular interest in giving up the Settlement but questioned whether the envisioned new community could be a moon of the Settlement or the Settlement a moon of the new community. Freeman may have regarded all of his work up until then as culminating in this project, as he recognised that over the years an ethos and 'a way of doing things' had been cultivated which would be essential in building the new community. He didn't want to lose this spiritual substance built up over the previous thirty years. Another factor integral to building such a community was for individuals to overcome the personal difficulties that 'so often devastate Anthroposophical work'. Freeman continued to search for a suitable property; his desire was to find a house with large grounds. He recognised that money would be the problem but 'if we let our needs be known; if people come to feel that we are capable of carrying through such an enterprise; if the Fates wish to spin this thread; then we shall sooner or later get what we want.'

Save Europe Now

An interesting episode in the history of the Settlement and in Freeman's biography was undoubtedly the 'German Refugee Crisis' at the end of the Second World War, which the material in the Settlement's archive sheds light on as the papers contain a wealth of letters received by members of the Settlement from German families who received the parcels sent there. These letters illustrate, firstly, the sacrifices made by those people who sent the parcels and the gratitude of those who received them. From the British perspective, only rationed food could be sent abroad so the parcels were made up of goods and items only obtainable on a ration card, so great sacrifices had to be made.

By the end of the war, the economic and social situation in Germany was dire. The economy was at a standstill and some of the cities were either partially destroyed or uninhabitable. Millions of people were rendered homeless by the destruction of the cities. In this context Victor Gollancz organized 'Save Europe Now' (SEN); a campaign to persuade the British Government to allow British people to send food parcels to Germany, which in the immediate post war period was forbidden. The SEN asked people to send a postcard if they were willing to give spare food or ration points from time to time and later there was an appeal for money to buy relief through existing organisations. The papers in the SES show how Freeman, his co-workers and the Sheffield District of United Nations Association organized the city into 'parishes' so that helpers could distribute tins to others who would then go out to collect money. This also included giving out instructions on how to send parcels to Germany.[46]

After receiving one of the parcels, a Wilhelm Fink in Stuttgart tells D. V. Barber that he had four children, one of whom was ill from malnutrition, but hoped that very soon vegetables would arrive from Holland and butter from Denmark. However, most of the population were in danger of suffering from malnutrition or even starvation as there appears to have been no coordinated plan to deal with the situation. Fink goes on to tell her the extent of black market dealing and racketeering. A pound of butter cost anywhere between 250 to 350 Reich Marks and a modest engagement ring normally costing 200 Reich Marks could be sold for upwards of 30,000 RM.

Another letter, dated April 1948, from Gerda von Heyderbrand describes how her two children were ill and weak and that milk was not available. They were therefore 'overjoyed with the biscuits and cans of milk they found in the food parcel.' Other items that were requested were sugar, syrup and honey, and according to a letter written by Ernst Lehrs, who was teaching at Michael Hall School in Sussex, combs were unobtainable and the people in Germany would be happy with the pocket combs costing four pence in Woolworths. It was also Lehrs who was active in supplying the names and addresses of those friends who were in great need.

The Golden Blade

For Freeman, one of his most significant achievements was the founding of the annual publication, *The Golden Blade*, together with Charles Davy. It is possible to discern from evidence in his papers that a publication based on Anthroposophy was something Freeman strived for long before the founding of *The Golden Blade* in 1949. From April 1924 to April 1925, Freeman published the monthly periodical *Facts and Dreams*, in which he included extracts from his diary under the heading: 'The Warden Winks at the World'. The stated purpose for publishing this was to proclaim in literary form the views of the Settlement. High hopes were placed on this becoming a widely read national independent magazine; however, due to financial difficulties it ceased publication after one year.

Freeman still published monthly newsletters, but it wasn't until he wrote to Charles Davy in 1948 that *The Golden Blade* came into existence. Davy tells us that it was entirely Freeman's idea to start a journal which he envisaged as reaching a wide public, and its aim was to bring 'the outlook of Anthroposophy to bear on issues of the day'. The first copy appeared in 1949, and in 1966 they handed the editorship over to Adam Bittleston and Gerald Rowe. Davy recalls that working together with Freeman was always friendly, and although Freeman was known to be pugnacious, prickly and obstinate, they worked together harmoniously. In fact he suggests that it was the intimate collaboration of their combined temperaments (all four) that gave *The Golden Blade* its distinction.

During the late 1940s and early 1950s Freeman became more active in the work of the Anthroposophical Society, and it was on his initiative that the Quarterly Symposium began. This was an important group founded on the weekend of the 19th – 21st of April 1947 at Clent, and it came out of the London-Sheffield conversation group whose members included Freeman, Adam Bittleston and Charles Davy. The aim of the Symposium was 'to gain an understanding of the tasks to which Anthroposophists are being called; to encourage the initiation of new activities and to arouse the interest of these activities carried out in these Isles.'

Retirement

During his retirement, after leaving the Settlement in 1955, Arnold began a campaign to do more for the elderly in Sheffield. In 1962 a committee was formed to establish Abbeyfield Houses for old age pensioners in Sheffield. This led to the formation in 1963 of the Abbeyfield Society with Freeman as its first chairman. In 1964 he published his booklet, *Unregarded Age in Corners Thrown,* in which he outlined in detail the problems facing older people who 'somewhere around the age of sixty-five', find themselves 'crossing a sort of unseen frontier'. The main problem, he wrote, and one which he wished to address was: how far can the community make good 'to those who have crossed the frontier into old age the things they are no longer able to provide for themselves?'

The basic solution, he argued, was to help as many elderly people to live on happily in their own homes with sufficient income, the right sort of house and to make sure they were 'known, watched, visited and given the help they need.' Before he published this booklet, the local Abbeyfield Society had, in March 1963, already purchased a large house at 148, Broomspring Lane and were in the process of converting it to be able to accommodate its first residents. The Abbeyfield Society, or 'Abbeyfield', as it is now called, was originally founded in 1955 by Richard Carr-Gormann, so it is assumed that Freeman was responsible for driving the initiative forward in Sheffield rather than participating in the founding of the national Society.

The Settlement buildings in Shipton Street were eventually pulled down in 1961 due to a road widening scheme and the new Warden, Christopher Boulton, continued the 'Settlement tradition' and moved to Meadowbank Road, where he built the Merlin Theatre and Arnold Freeman Hall. This establishment still exists and is run and managed by Freeman College and Brantwood Specialist School, which are part of the Ruskin Mill Trust, a pioneering educational charity with an international reputation for realising the potential of young people with special needs.

At the age of sixty-nine Freeman moved to Michaelmas Cottage, Gooseham in Cornwall, a place very near to his heart. He knew all the best walks, went searching for circular patterns of stones and maintained an avid interest in botany. He died in March 1972 at the age of eighty-six and was cremated at Barnstaple Crematorium.

The final word should be given to his former student, Emily Neill:

Mr Freeman is the modern version of the Friar. He has the fire of the Dominican, his love of knowledge; his thirst for the things of the spirit. With these he combines the Franciscan's sympathetic affection for his fellow men. It is this mixture that makes him an inspiring teacher.

Final Reflections

Our birth is but a sleep and a forgetting;
The Soul that rises with us, our life's Star,
Hath had elsewhere its setting,
And cometh from afar;
Not in entire forgetfulness,
And not in utter nakedness,
But trailing clouds of glory do we come,
From God, who is our home.
(Wordsworth: 'Intimations of Immortality')

Much the same as our fingerprints or the irises of our eyes, everyone's biography is unique. Every single one of us experiences the world differently; we all see the physical world from a different perspective. As I write this, that makes approximately 7.8 billion unique lives and different perspectives on life. Additionally, we all have our own way of interpreting the experiences that happen to us on a daily basis; our own way of expressing ourselves, our own voice, our own problems and obstacles to overcome and our own special questions. Modern science tells us that life on this planet is a purposeless product of probabilities in a universe that is indifferent to our existence.

Arnold James Freeman would have thought very differently about the purpose of life. From his study into the 'occult sciences' such as Theosophy and Anthroposophy, he would have been convinced that our life is a story we have created before birth that unfolds over the course of our lifetime. Much as in William Wordsworth's 'Intimations of Immortality', AJF thought that the human spirit existed before birth in the spiritual world, and it is *that* world which is our true home.

This is not the definitive biography of Arnold James Freeman. There is an abundance of material still available to research and write about, and it would probably take many years of work for someone to explore all the stories that could be told about him, his extended family, his wide circle of friends and acquaintances, and the numerous activities he undertook during his very full life. It was not my intention in writing this life of AJF to portray him as either a saint or a tyrant – or by any other designation to be found between these two extremes. I have tried instead to leave it up to the reader's own judgement what sort of person Freeman was. While there were a number of instances in which it would have been possible to cast aspersions on his character especially, for example, in his handling of the 1925 attempt to oust him as warden of the Settlement, there are at least as many instances that speak to his finer qualities: compassion, courage and a zeal for social justice.

During my research, which included conversations with family and friends who knew him, I discovered mainly positive aspects of his personality rather than any negative ones. The various press cuttings I consulted were surprisingly positive about him, some, however, contained a whiff of mockery or negativity. One journalist questioned his vision to build the Kingdom of God on Shipton Street by saying that after the Settlement was demolished 'Kelvin Flats were built on the site instead'.

It was this vision, however, and Freeman's philosophy that education is 'an inner spiritual process, which the State is no more competent to run than a wolf is to run a garden', that earned him the more dubious title of 'Philosopher of the Dark Streets'. He waged a unique campaign, says another journalist, against ignorance in his 'radical Ruskin-like organisation that was devoted to improving the spiritual welfare of the working (or more often un-working) man'. The education that he cultivated was not just about the dissemination of knowledge, but more about his desire to endow his students with capacities for self-development that underpinned his belief that education is the most revolutionary force in existence. John Roberts produced a piece of writing from a long-standing member of the settlement that summarises everything positive that could be said about AJF and the impact he had on the City of Sheffield:

AJF was a leaven, a ferment in the doleful unemployed years of the
1920s. He was an element in the hopeless, dreary district of Shipton
Street. Many hundreds and perhaps thousands of people in
Sheffield have had their mental, spiritual and psychological
horizons widened by their contact with him and his infectious
enthusiasm for the arts and literature of our day and the days of the
Middle Ages or Ancient Greece. He acted as guide, counsellor and
friend to a constant stream of people who found their way to his
minute Quiet Room at the top of the perilous stairs of Shipton
Street… there was undoubtedly a magical element about the
Settlement derived directly from AJF… the Settlement was Arnold
Freeman purely and simply.

I must also mention Grace Hoy, who wrote about Freeman in her book
Inwardly Limitless. She wrote it from the perspective of someone who
worked very closely with Freeman and who identified him as the 'heartbeat'
of the Settlement. This statement is very true, as without Freeman the
Settlement would not have been what it was and without him there would
be no Sheffield Repertory Theatre, and hundreds, if not thousands, of
people would have been deprived of the cultural impulse beating out from
Shipton Street. Her book proved to be an excellent starting point for me
when I set out to write this biography. I learned much about the context
within which he worked; got to know how the Settlement functioned and
above all I developed a 'feeling' for the character of Freeman. But Freeman
seems not to have been the paragon of virtue Hoy recalls in her book,
as we can see from the extraordinary evidence in his diaries. Many times
throughout his life he never seemed really settled; there was an inner disso-
nance about the course his life was taking. It is as though he was never really
satisfied; not in his love life; his work life or in his personal relationships.
Examples of this are found in his relationships with Winifred, Juliet and
above all Nora. As mentioned above, his relationship and marriage to Nora
was not ideal. Even when he found employment in the WEA, which gave
him great joy, he dreamed of becoming a great writer. What manifested
itself outwardly in his unconstrained, prickly, obstinate, more negative part

of his character was a mirror image of his inner life, and although I would suggest that he had a good feeling for his destiny, he struggled inwardly to make sense of what came towards him.

A positive facet of Arnold's character, which is indisputable, was his social conscience and his fierce devotion to helping others. Freeman believed in the unlimited capacity of the human being to develop spiritually, to develop the skills of deep listening, to develop the quality of profound empathy for all the individuals we meet on a daily basis, irrespective of gender, race, social position, ethnicity or creed. Indeed, he thought we all have the responsibility to develop these capacities in this lifetime, in order to make the world a better place. AJF always challenged people to cultivate independent thought, and he rejected the idea that there are matters over which an ordinary person has no control. We are all capable of awakening the faculties that slumber in our souls to become fuller, finer, more rounded human beings, to better place ourselves at the service of others. One might question the quality of Freeman's adherence to Anthroposophy, but we can't dispute the fact he dedicated his whole life to helping and educating others, as part of his vision for the future of humanity. This was the true Arnold James Freeman, always striving, always helping and always believing in the uniqueness of each individual human being.

Acknowledgements

In the writing and research of this biography I have benefitted from the generosity of many people. My starting point was a visit in 2007 to the Special Collections at the University of Sheffield, and I would like to thank Jackie Hodgson and her team for their expertise and patience in helping me with my initial exploration of the Sheffield Educational Settlement Papers. My next debt of gratitude goes to the late Philip Martyn who gave a generous grant to the University of Sheffield which allowed us to put the papers in good order. The family of Arnold James Freeman loaned me the diaries for an exceptionally long time so I would like to thank Pearl Myers for her generosity and Pam Freeman and other family members for help with the photographs. Thanks to John Lines for providing me with the photograph of the Lines family. Mr Cheney, Archivist at the Haberdashers' Boys' School, sent me copious documents about Freeman and his time there. I have given lectures on Freeman in various places over the past few years, including Freeman College in Sheffield, the Anthroposophical Group in Sheffield and Emerson College in Forest Row, East Sussex. I thank all members of staff at these institutions for hosting me but especially Jeremy Smith at Emerson, Aonghus Gordon OBE at Ruskin Mill Trust and Steve Roberts in Sheffield. I am extremely grateful to Richard Masters and the Trustees of the Hermes Trust, and John Pickin and the Trustees of the Christopher Francis Trust, for giving Wynstones Press a grant towards the publication of this book. There are numerous other individuals who have helped me in one way or another over the past few years including William and Jacob Forward, but I would especially like to thank Jacob who read the whole book in various drafts and gave expert editorial advice and encouragement in the final stages prior to publication.

Notes

As a large part of the research for this book was carried out during the 2020/2021 Covid 19 pandemic, there are many references to Websites rather than books and journal articles as access to libraries was restricted.

1. For a fuller description of the Papers see:
   https://www.sheffield.ac.uk/library/special/polopoly_fs/1.557694!/file/SheffieldEducationalSettlement.pdf.
   Gibson, Kenneth (2010), *Adam Bittleston: His Work, Life and Thought*, Edinburgh: Floris Books.

2. Roberts, John (1961), *The Sheffield Educational Settlement (1918-1955)*, University of Sheffield: Certificate of Education dissertation.

3. I am indebted to the articles written by David Martin (1999), *Arnold Freeman and the Sheffield Educational Settlement*, Transactions of the Hunter Archaeological Society, Volume 20, pp. 71-80, and his article on Freeman in the Dictionary of Labour Biography, 1993 pp. 91-95.

4. Davy, Charles (1972), *Obituary of Arnold Freeman*, Anthroposophical Movement, Volume 49, No. 3.

5. Hoy, Grace, (No Date), *Inwardly Limitless: 19th Century Reformers, The University Settlement Movement and Education by Magic at the Sheffield Educational Settlement under Arnold Freeman*, Privately Printed: Truro.

6. Charles Booth's *Inquiry into the Life and Labour of the People in London*, undertaken between 1886 and 1903 and eventually published in 17 volumes in 1902/1903 by Macmillan, London. Seebohm Rowntree carried out his survey into poverty in York which was published as: *Poverty, A Study of Town Life* (1901).

7.   https://ukcensusonline.com/census/1911/

8.   The quote that Freeman is probably referring to here is: 'Find the thing you want to do most intensely, make sure that's it, and do it with all your might. If you live, well and good. If you die, well and good. Your purpose is done.'

9.   Bloxham, Mike (2004), *The Green Casanova: An Affectionate Biography of Peter Freeman, Maverick MP*, Aberystwyth: Y Lolfa

10.   Much of the information on Freeman's school years was provided by Mr Cheney the Archivist at the Haberdashers' Boys' School.

11.   For more information on this see: https://www.legislation.gov.uk/ukpga/Vict/52-53/72/contents/enacted

12.   I consulted numerous sources for the background on the Welsh Revival including: The Bible College of Wales: https://www.bcwales.org/1904-welsh-revival

13.   Sidney Ball was another influential individual in Freeman's life. He was a senior tutor at Oxford and was so dedicated to socialism that he earned himself the name 'the Socialist Don'. He was also a member of the Fabian Society and an early supporter of the Workers Educational Association. See the 2004 article by F. S. Lee in the Oxford Dictionary of National Biography, https://doi.org/10.1093/ref:odnb/38749

14.   For background information on the Keswick Conferences see: https://keswickministries.org/history/

15.   There are various pieces of writing available online about this school but see especially: Manton, Kevin (1997), Establishing the fellowship: Harry Lowerison and Ruskin School Home, a turn-of-the-century socialist and his educational experiment, *Journal of the History of Education Society, Volume 26.*

16.   For more on Lawson see: Bythell, Duncan (2004), Lawson, John James [Jack], Baron Lawson, Oxford Dictionary of National Biography, https://doi.org/10.1093/ref:odnb/47371

17.   For information on GBS I used the 3-volume biography by Michael Holroyd published by Chatto and Windus, 1988.

18. This Play was first performed on May 12th 1908 at the Haymarket Theatre in London.

19. Lynn, Denise M. (2021), *Where Is Juliet Stuart Poyntz?: Gender, Spycraft, and Anti-Stalinism in the Early Cold War – Culture and Politics in the Cold War and Beyond*, University of Massachusetts Press. I would like to thank Denise for providing me with this information before the publication of her book. A video of Denise talking about her book can be found at: https://vimeo.com/541622180.
    See also: Tresca, Carlo (1938), *Where is Juliet Stuart Poyntz?* New York: The Modern Monthly, Volume 10, No. 11, pp. 12-13.

20. The American Guru TK, his partner Florence Huntley and Freeman's friend Sean Williams are discussed in more detail in Chapter 6.

21. Eustace Hamilton Miles was an award winning tennis payer, Olympic medalist, vegetarian and restaurant owner. His vegetarian restaurant at the western end of Covent Garden was one of the most famous restaurants in Edwardian London. Freeman dined there on many occasions.

22. Graham Wallas was a socialist, educational psychologist, a cofounder of the LSE and a close co-worker of the Webbs.

23. For the history of the Society of Psychical Research see their website at: https://www.spr.ac.uk/about/our-history

24. See the Website at: https://www.attackingthedevil.co.uk/spiritualism/

25. Stead, W. T. (1910), *The River of Death*, E. W. Cole Book Arcade, Melbourne, Australia, p.6.

26. There are numerous publications on the Occult Revival in the Victorian and Edwardian era. See, for example: Butler, Alison (2011), *Victorian Occultism and the Making of Modern Magic: Invoking Tradition* (Palgrave Historical Studies in Witchcraft and Magic), Palgrave Macmillan. See Also: Owen, Alex (2007), *The Place of Enchantment: British Occultism and the Culture of the Modern*, University of Chicago Press.

27. West, Sylvester A (2010), *TK and The Great Work in America: An Amazing Case of Masonic Fraud*, New Orleans: Cornerstone Books, (First published in Chicago in 1918 with the subtitle: *A Defense of*

the True and Ancient School of Spiritual Light.)

28. For this chapter I have used various online sources, including the entries for Sidney and Beatrice Webb in the Oxford Dictionary of National Biography, the online sources at the London School of Economics (LSE) and various writings and reviews published by the Fabian Society. See also the online resources at the LSE Website including the diaries of Beatrice Webb: https://digital.library.lse.ac.uk/objects/lse:six767gol

29. He did, however, continue lecturing on the Minority Report. See the extensive reports of two of his lectures in: The South Wales Gazette, November 10th, 1911.

30. Lunn, Pam (2007), *Woodbrooke in Wider Context: The Enduring Thread of Adult Education*, Quaker Studies, Volume 11, 2, pp. 204-223.

31. Herbert Albert Laurens Fisher (1865-1940) OM PC FRS FBA was an English historian, educator, and Liberal politician. He served as President of the Board of Education in David Lloyd George's 1916 to 1922 coalition. See also: Judge, Harry (2006), *H.A.L. Fisher: Scholar and Minister*, Oxford Review of Education, Volume 32, No 1, pp.5-21. The University Extension Movement was founded to enable working men and women to gain access to higher education. All tutors were vetted for their qualifications and their sympathy towards working men and women.

32. Much of the information on Hayward has been taken from: Bhimani, Nazlin (2015), F. H. Hayward (1872-1954), *A Forgotten Educationalist or an Educational Failure? Moral Education and Education for Citizenship in England.* Masters Thesis, University College London: Institute of Education.

33. Eagles, Stuart (2015), *Political Legacies in: The Cambridge Companion to John Ruskin*, edited by O'Gorman, Francis, pp. 249-262, Cambridge: Cambridge University Press.

34. See: Atwood, S. E. (2008), 'John Ruskin on Education', *The encyclopedia of pedagogy and informal education.* [https://infed.org/mobi/john-ruskin-on-education.)

35. Published as a booklet in 1922 with a Foreword by Freeman: Steiner, Rudolf (1922), *Spiritual Life, Civil Rights, Industrial Economy*, London: Anthroposophical Publishing Company.

36. See: Villeneuve, Crispian (2004), *Rudolf Steiner in Britain: A Documentation of his Ten Visits, Volume 2, 1922-1925*, Forest Row: Temple Lodge Publishing and Paull, John (2011), Rudolf Steiner and the Oxford Conference: The Birth of Waldorf Education in Britain, *European Journal of Educational Studies*, Volume 3, 1, pp. 53-66.

37. Most of the information that follows about the Settlement is taken from various sources in the Settlement papers and Freeman, Mark (2002), *No Finer School Than a Settlement, The Development of the Educational Settlement Movement*, History of Education, Volume 31, 2, pp. 245-262.

38. For this section I consulted: Seed, Alec T (1959), *The Sheffield Repertory Theatre: A History*, Sheffield: The Sheffield Repertory Company and the many and various documents in the Settlement Papers.

39. See the New York Public Library Archive for biographical information on Prentice: https://archives.nypl.org/the/21400

40. *Sheffield Evening Telegraph*, 31st March 1921.

41. The following is based on Mark Freeman's excellent article: Freeman, Mark (2013), 'An Advanced Type of Democracy?' *Governance and Politics in Adult Education c. 1918-1930*. History of Education, Volume. 42, No. 1, pp. 45-69. There are also many documents in the SES papers that I consulted to address this complex issue.

42. Most of the biographical information on Rootham and Sitwell in this section is taken from: Greene, Richard (2011), *Edith Sitwell: Avant Garde Poet, English Genius*, London: Virago.

43. For a fuller discussion of this and the relevant references see: Jeremy Smith: https://anthropopper.com/tag/marilyn-monroe/

44. https://www.visitnesm.org.uk/post/remembering-the-sheffield-blitz

45. Most of the following section on König and the plans for a school in Sheffield is based on documents found in the SES papers.

46. For a fuller academic discussion of the post-war refugee crisis see: Frank, Matthew (2006), *The New Morality – Victor Gollancz, 'Save Europe Now' and the German Refugee Crisis, 1945-46*, Twentieth Century British History, Volume 17, 2, pp. 230-256. See also the book written and published by Victor Gollancz, *In Darkest Germany* (1947), which is an account of his six-week visit to Germany in 1946.

The Writings and Publications of Arnold James Freeman

Single-Authored

(1911), 'The Place of Charge and Recovery in the Minority Report of the Royal Commission on the Poor Laws'. *The Economic Journal*, Vol. 21, Issue 82.

(1914), *An Investigation into the causes that render large numbers of Boys unable to obtain Employment on reaching Early Manhood with special reference to the conditions of Boy Life and Labour in Birmingham*, (Oxford BLitt).

(1914), *Boy Life and Labour: The Manufacture of Inefficiency*, London: P. S. King & Son Ltd.

(1914), *An Introduction to the Study of Social Problems*, London: Worker's Educational Association.

(1919), *How to Avoid a Revolution*, London: G. Allen and Unwin.

(1920), *Education Through Settlements*, London: G. Allen and Unwin.

(1927), *Rudolf Steiner and the Crisis in Human Affairs*, Sheffield: Sheffield Educational Settlement.

(1936), *The Golden Book of the Settlement and Hollowford*, Sheffield: Sheffield Educational Settlement.

(1942), *A Workable and Desirable World*, Sheffield: Sheffield Educational Settlement.

(1944), *Who was Rudolf Steiner, What is Anthroposophy?* Sheffield: Sheffield Educational Settlement.

(1947), *Goethe and Steiner*, Sheffield: Sheffield Educational Settlement.

(1952), 'Rudolf Steiner and the Theatre', *The Golden Blade*, London.

(1949), 'Darwinism and Dreams', *The Golden Blade*, London

(1954), *The Riddle of Goethe's Faust*, Sheffield: Sheffield Educational Settlement.

(1956), *Self-Observation: An Introduction to Rudolf Steiner's Philosophy of Spiritual Activity*, London: Anthroposophical Publishing Company.

(1957), *Meditation Under the Guidance of Rudolf Steiner*, Sheffield: Sheffield Educational Settlement.

(1958), *Rudolf Steiner's Message to Mankind*, East Grinstead: New Knowledge Books.

(1963), *What Rudolf Steiner says Concerning Initiation and Meditation*, Sheffield: Sheffield Educational Settlement.

(1964), *Unregarded Age in Corners Thrown*, Sheffield: Centre for Research, Publicity and Information about the Old Age Problem in Sheffield.

(1966), *Why I am a 'Steinerian'*, Privately Published.

Joint Authorship

Freeman, A. J; Beckett-Overy, H; Hastings, S, 'The Medical Proposals of the Minority Report: A Plea to the Medical Profession', *The Lancet*, 23rd July 1910, pp. 229-233.

AJF and Webb, Sidney (1912), *Seasonal Trades*, London: Constable.

AJF and Bernard Henderson (1915), *A Manual on Essay Writing for Students of the Workers' Educational Association*, London: WEA.

AJF and Webb, Sidney (1916), *Great Britain After the War*, London: G. Allen and Unwin.

AJF and Cole, G.D.H, (Eds.) (1918), *The Education Year Book*, London: WEA.

AJF and Hayward, F. H, (1919), *The Spiritual Foundations of Reconstruction: A Plea for New Educational Methods*, London: P. S. King & Son Ltd.

AJF and Cecil, H; Davies, H; Dodson, F; Lewis, E; Pinner, J.S, (1919), *Brightest England and the Way In*, London: G. Allen and Unwin.

AJF with members of the St. Philip's settlement education and economics research society, Sheffield (1919), *The Equipment of the Workers*, London: G. Allen and Unwin.

AJF and Viccars, A (Eds.), (1920 and 1921), *The Adult School Handbook*.

Plays

St. Paul (1938).

Winning the War (1940).

The Dream Maiden.

Wynstones Press

publishes and distributes a range of
Books, Advent Calendars, Cards and Prints.
For further information please see:

www.wynstonespress.com
info@wynstonespress.com